The
LOVE *of*
SCOTLAND

THE LOVE OF

SCOTLAND

Leslie Gardiner

octopus

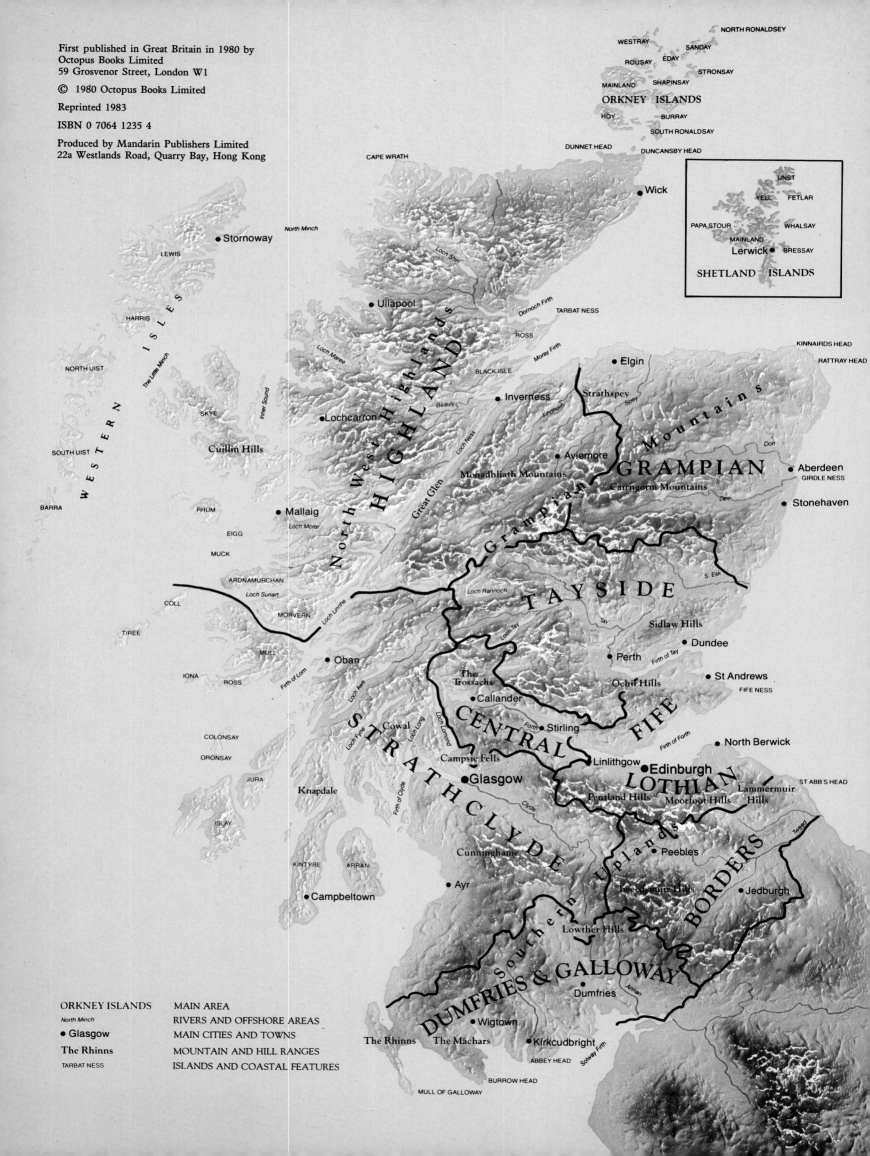

First published in Great Britain in 1980 by
Octopus Books Limited
59 Grosvenor Street, London W1

© 1980 Octopus Books Limited

Reprinted 1983

ISBN 0 7064 1235 4

Produced by Mandarin Publishers Limited
22a Westlands Road, Quarry Bay, Hong Kong

ORKNEY ISLANDS   MAIN AREA
North Minch   RIVERS AND OFFSHORE AREAS
● Glasgow   MAIN CITIES AND TOWNS
The Rhinns   MOUNTAIN AND HILL RANGES
TARBAT NESS   ISLANDS AND COASTAL FEATURES

CONTENTS

The publishers wish to thank the Scottish Tourist Board for its
assistance in providing the majority of the photographs in this book.

Title Rannoch Moor in the western Highlands covers
518 sq km (200 sq miles) of desolate country.

Half-title A lone piper, one of Scotland's many symbols.

INTRODUCTION

On the map or from the air Scotland resembles an uncompleted jigsaw puzzle, a puzzle whose northernmost pieces overlap the latitude of Greenland and the southernmost the latitude of Omsk. Climate and botany, however, reflect little of the extremes of those places.

Scotland is about the size of Belgium and the Netherlands together, with about one-fifth of their combined populations. If you set out from London to travel the length of Great Britain, you would reach Scotland at the midpoint of your journey, with the most tortuous half of the trip to come.

The country is divided broadly into Highlands, a group of massifs, moors, ravines and torrents, and Lowlands, which are not in fact low but are mainly a series of smooth hills and pastures intersected by river valleys and belts of manufacturing towns. On the eastern seaboard, cliffs and headlands stand guard over river estuaries (*firths*) and angular bays. The west coast is split into ragged promontories and inland seas (*sea lochs*) which overlook a panorama of 700 islands. Three distinct groups of islands, Orkney and Shetland in the north and the Outer Hebrides in the north-west, are rich in Norse memories. The tiny uninhabited isles of St Kilda and Rockall lie beyond the blue Atlantic horizon, 180 km (112 miles) and 470 km (292 miles) respectively from the Scottish mainland.

As the beating of Atlantic rollers formed the seascape, so the harsh weathering of native rock and the passage of glaciers shaped the landscape: the attractive pinks and greys of sandstone and granite hills, Scott's 'darksome glens and gleaming lochs', and the crag-and-tail formations on which were built the superb fortresses of Stirling and Edinburgh. These impressive formations occurred where ice-rivers hit impregnable rock. The ice divided and flowed round the rock, leaving behind a diminishing trail of rubble.

The land has two natural, geological divisions: the narrow neck of land, only 45 km (28 miles) from sea to sea, between the Firth of Forth and Firth of Clyde, and the 93-km (58-mile) corridor between Inverness and Fort William. The latter comprises three riverine lochs, among them Loch Ness, which makes almost a natural canal. The engineer Thomas Telford started improving this natural waterway with locks and sluices in 1803, and it opened as the Caledonian Canal 44 years later.

A third natural divide manifests itself in occasional slight earth tremors around Comrie in Perthshire and in sudden sharp cascades on north-south rivers. This is the Highland Line, running roughly from Stonehaven to Rothesay, a geological fault which a few million years ago caused the central regions of Scotland to sink away from the Highlands.

The title of this book expresses a characteristic of the Scottish people. Sir Walter Scott, supreme propagandist for the nation, and a host of patriotic writers since his time have stressed the superiority of all things Scottish: the scenery, Scottish determination and courage, and Scottish law, education and football. Sceptical non-Scots should beware; these extravagant claims are frequently all too true. Scotland's scenery is spectacular, though its greatest river is but a rivulet and the highest mountain but a hill on the world scale. Scottish history and legend are stormy and dramatic, as the playwrights Shakespeare and Schiller and the composers Donizetti and Bellini recognized. Sensitive 19th-century observers such as Jules Verne, Hans Andersen, Mendelssohn, Chopin, Ruskin, Bret Harte, Wordsworth and Washington Irving visited Scotland to see if Scott's 'Caledonia stern and wild' really existed. They went home enchanted by the grandeur of the Highlands, the colour harmonies of forest and loch, the fairytale castles, the gloomy citadels and the wildlife. They were charmed even by the weather which capriciously scatters the clouds, mists and slanting sunshine integral to the Scottish landscape.

Some irresistible element infuses everything Scotland offers us. There may be other countries whose fighting men wear skirts, whose music comes from a bag of wind, whose peasant diet includes a lump of offal and onions, and whose deepwater lakes have their mythical monsters. But for most people the kilt, the bagpipes, the haggis and the Loch Ness monster evoke the spirit of Scotland.

Industrialization has changed some of the scenes which Scott made famous. Scotland has its urban sprawls and, in the once-idyllic north-east, a growing oil industry. However, over broad tracts of mainland and on every island the visitor may still travel on peaceful, well-made roads and networks of hill and forest trails such as few other countries possess.

No part of the mainland is more than 64 km (40 miles) from the sea. This fact has influenced Scotland's history as much as its proximity to a larger, richer neighbour, England. Romantics trace Scotland's historical beginnings to Scota, daughter of a Biblical pharaoh. To successive expansionist powers—the Romans, the Norsemen and the Anglo-Saxons—Scotland was little more than a trouble-spot. Until the 14th century the organization of its monarchy was primitive and the one real dynasty, the Stuarts, brought little but internal and external anguish until union with England in 1707 settled most quarrels. Jacobite rebellions in 1715 and 1745 account for some picturesque legends in modern Scotland, but its subsequent history was generally speaking the history of Great Britain, of which it remains a part.

The Scots as a nation are proud and parochial and resolutely opposed to any movement which threatens their independence. In rural communities there is a strong attachment to old values and moral standards. Religious bigotry is not unknown, but class distinctions in Scotland are less emphatic than in England. The characteristics one associates with the typical Scot are fortitude and obduracy, thrift and a keen business instinct; and a love of Scotland.

Right Balmoral Castle, Scottish retreat of the British Royal Family, lies west of Aberdeen, in Grampian region.

LOTHIAN

Previous page A view of the Palace of Holyroodhouse with Arthur's Seat beyond. King James IV began the present palace, based on a guesthouse of a former Abbey, but most of the buildings that stand today were built for Charles II. Arthur's Seat is an extinct volcano from which there is a splendid view of the city.

Above The clock on the tower of the North British hotel above Edinburgh's Waverley station is kept five minutes fast as encouragement to those rushing for a train. From a viewpoint on the Calton Hill, the Gothic spires of central Edinburgh rise above Princes Street. This is said to be the only main street in Europe without a double row of shops, for the south side is all gardens. The nearest spire on the left is the Scott Monument, raised above an effigy of the novelist.

Right Participants in the Tattoo on the esplanade of Edinburgh Castle parade for the final salute after an evening performance. The Military Tattoo, given twice nightly during the three-week Edinburgh International Festival of Music, Drama and the Arts (August–September), has proved itself very popular and a great financial success since it began in 1947. The programme is built around displays by the best of regimental, cavalry, dance and acrobatic troupes from countries round the world. They make dramatic entrances and exits by way of the drawbridge and portcullis which are still the only means of access to the castle. Audiences are multinational like the performers, but the majority of spectators are Scots. The most enthusiastic acclaim is usually reserved for the Highland dancers and the massed pipe bands of the Highland regiments. Lighting effects and the batteries and ramparts of the old sturdy citadel provide memorable backcloths for the events. The climax of the spectacle is a solitary piper playing a lament, spotlit on a high tower while all the castle rock is darkened.

Lothian region, comprising the three counties of West Lothian, Midlothian and East Lothian on the southern shores of the Firth of Forth, is the most cosmopolitan of Scottish regions, partly because it was once part of Anglo-Saxon Northumbria (Lothian suggests Lud, a semi-mythical British king whose name crops up in several Saxon place-names). Its port of Leith has historic links with the continent of Europe, and most newcomers to Scotland enter by way of its coastal routes, the A1 London-Edinburgh highway or the mainline King's Cross-Waverley railway. Lothian region also embraces Edinburgh, seat of kings, centre of Scottish government, banking and insurance capital, hotbed of lawyers and architects, festival city of international renown, and place of residence of English and foreign expatriates.

Edinburgh, gathered round its castle crag, has one of the most romantic situations of any city in the world. The panorama it surveys is a foretaste of the Highlands—and of the islands too, for Edinburgh's footstool is Inchkeith in the Forth. This is the spot where an early Stuart king marooned two infants with a deaf-and-dumb nurse to determine what was the original language of mankind. When the children were five years old philosophers agreed that they spoke 'guid Ebrew'. The eastern prospects of the city range over the Bass Rock.

Edinburgh's ancient heart spreads over both sides of the 'Royal Mile', the descending thoroughfare which connects the castle with the Palace of Holyroodhouse. This area is medieval and Frenchified, with crow-stepped gables, wrought-ironwork, steep arcades, a corridor of craft shops, museums and antique businesses. Until quite recently it was a disreputable quarter. The so-called New Town (18th-century), adjoining the Old, is an urban planning masterpiece of terraces, squares and circuses built from local granite, a rectilinear tartan in black and grey which continues to mediate between changing architectural fashions. Beyond New Town and Old, the suburban sprawl is dotted here and there by a ruined castle, an old packhorse bridge or a gaunt mansion, each with a tale of the past, frequently of a murderous and treacherous kind.

Moments of history spring to life in the 13th–15th-century castles of the Lothian shore, among them Blackness, Dundas, Dirleton, Tantallon and Dunbar. 'Ding doon Tantallon! Mak' a brig to the Bass!' says the ancient proverb, applied to someone who proposes an impossible feat. Cramond Brig and Linlithgow Palace proclaim the old royal route to the west. Dunbar's tottering red sandstone fortress and Haddington's venerable church called 'Lamp of Lothian' typify the fundamental elements of Lothian Heritage: war and religion.

The Midlothian coalfield extends well into East Lothian's farmland and some of the submarine workings link up with the Fife coalfields across the Forth. Streams which enter the firth at Cramond, Leith and Musselburgh have papermaking traditions. Edinburgh itself has manufacturing concerns, based on rubber, milling, printing and brewing.

Visitors in search of scenic or antiquarian features cannot go far wrong around Edinburgh or Linlithgow, around Haddington, the market centre of East Lothian, or the coastal town of Dunbar, which incidentally boasts the best sunshine record in Scotland. The eastern shores on the rapidly broadening firth are an uninterrupted string of golf courses, nature reserves and bird sanctuaries. Some of the small communities, such as Aberlady, Gullane and North Berwick, wear a genteel air, and have their roots firmly embedded in history. A few stone-built villages in the foothills of Lammermuir contend for the title of Scotland's prettiest.

Stately homes survive: the large Adam pile of Hopetoun (Marquess of Linlithgow); the Victorian house of Dalmeny (Earl of Rosebery), noted for its snowdrop woods and its trees planted by royalty dead and gone; Lennoxlove (Duke of Hamilton), a photogenic fortified country house dating back 500 years; and Tyninghame (Earl of Haddington) with its 12th-century Romanesque chapel—Lothian has long been the seedbed of Lowland gentility.

The scenic districts are spread beside minor roads that are like Highland passes in miniature. Trout streams gush through heather-covered valleys. The coloured hills, patterned with grass, heather and bracken echo to the cries of grouse, pheasant, lapwing and curlew. Hare and deer are common. These lonely hills and dales begin less than half an hour by road from Edinburgh.

SCOTTISH KINGS AND QUEENS

From a darker Dark Age than most other lands of western Europe had known, the people of Scotland emerged in about AD 600 as four tribal peoples. These were the Picts in the north, the Scots in the west, the Britons in the south-west and the Angles, or English, in the south-east. Christianity and a common enemy, the Norsemen, helped unite them. Kenneth MacAlpin, the Scoto-Pict chieftain, is sometimes called the first king of Scotland (843). Stricter genealogies, however, begin with Malcolm Canmore ('Great Head') in 1057, immediately after the events which Shakespeare dramatized in *Macbeth*. For 200 years the kingdom wavered between the warring Atholl and Moray lines of the old MacAlpin dynasty. The monarchy was weak and its organization rudimentary, until royal marriages with Englishwomen and the adoption of Anglo-Norman feudal ideas brought stability, at the cost of making Scotland a client state of England. King Robert I (the Bruce) and his partisan brigades finally liberated Scotland in 1328. His daughter's son, Robert II (1371-90), began the long Stuart dynasty. Most of its eleven kings, three queens and two pretenders died violently or miserably in campaigns against the English, or in struggles to assert their authority over unruly barons and churchmen. The surname Stuart, or Stewart, comes from Walter, son-in-law of the Bruce, father of Robert II and High Steward of Scotland. The defeat in 1746 of the Young Pretender (whom his adherents styled King Charles III) marked the effective end of the dynasty. But the British royal family, the House of Windsor, is in direct descent from Walter the Steward of Scotland, as are most surviving royal houses, ruling or in exile, of Europe today.

Above Robert the Bruce was crown King of Scotland in 1306. He rallied the feuding people of Scotland to fight and win against their common enemy, the English, at Bannockburn in 1314. The statue above is in Stirling, Central.

Left Almost as much romantic ink has been spilled over Mary Queen of Scots as over her great-great-great-grandson Prince Charles Edward, but objective eyes see her as a sharp and wilful schemer. She succeeded to the Scottish throne when only a few hours old. Later she was sent to France for safety and at 16 married the Dauphin (crown prince). Her French mother ruled Scotland on behalf of the French king, while the Protestant agitator, Knox, thundered against the 'monstrous regiment of women'. Taking over her realm as a bewitching widow of 18, Mary faced the irreconcilable tasks of placating Elizabeth of England (whom she hoped to succeed) and simultaneously restoring Catholicism to Britain. This job was made no easier by her rash second and third marriages. Driven from Scotland, she became Elizabeth's captive in 1568 and was beheaded for treason in 1587, having spent nearly half her life in prison. This painting is attributed to P. Oudry, after Nicholas Hilliard, 1578.

Right James VI of Scotland, son of Mary Queen of Scots, united two crowns when he became James I of England on the death of Elizabeth in 1603. The painting is by Daniel Mytens.

13

The Forth Railway Bridge is 2·5 km (1·5 miles) long. It was designed by Benjamin Baker and opened in 1890. The proportions of the bridge are so elegant that it is necessary to stand underneath it to appreciate that the cantilevers are higher than St Paul's dome in London and that a full-sized train could run down the tubular struts. Baker also built dams at Aswan in Egypt, part of London's underground railway and a tunnel under the Hudson River, New York. In 1964, Scotland acquired its first long-span suspension bridge 3 km (2 miles) upstream, a link across the river for the Edinburgh-Perth motorway. While building the rail bridge, 56 men lost their lives; on the road bridge, only one. As a work of civil engineering, the latter steals the limelight, but the older Forth Bridge still holds its course, shortening the railway route to the north.

Below On the river bank at Haddington, where swans feed, stands the 'Lamp of Lothian', St Mary's parish church. This remained a flickering beacon of rustic piety and simple faith through the irreligious phases of Lothian history. Monolithic gravestones, pink and grey from the sandstone and granite substratum, are a feature of Lothian churchyards. The bas-reliefs they bear (strange devices, anchors and portrayals of farming activities) are a calendar of social history through the ages. Haddington was a royal burgh, a birthplace of kings, and the last stop before Edinburgh on the Great North Road from London in coaching days. It became a petrified antique when the railways came and the main-line trains bypassed it. Now many of its buildings have been expertly restored.

Right Some people suggest that Tantallon in East Lothian, and not Tintagel in Cornwall, is the castle where King Arthur and the Knights of the Round Table met. Tantallon, however, is not quite as old as that. The Black Douglas reared this most forbidding of coastal strongholds in the 15th century, giving it (as the geologist Hugh Miller has written) 'three sides of rock-like wall and one of wall-like rock'.

BORDERS

Previous page Net fishermen at work beside the Union suspension bridge near Berwick-upon-Tweed. Some of Europe's finest salmon are born in the Tweed and return in spring to spawn in their native pools.

Above Every summer since 1599 the Braw Lad with his Lass and retainers has ridden out and about in Galashiels in a week-long celebration of the granting of a royal charter. This is a manifestation of civic pride in which outsiders cannot properly participate. Otherwise, Galashiels is the least introverted of the conservative 'twinset towns'. It has the only Scottish textile college and is the focus of a plan to repopulate the Tweed valley with 25,000 newcomers who will live and work in this beautiful area.

Right In the heart of Scott's beloved Borderland, a gravel sweep on a hilltop beside the Earlston-Dryburgh road has been designated *Scott's View*. The panoramic view embraces a score of towers, hills and habitations enshrined in literature and embraced by the Tweed's crescent bends. The background humps are the Eildon hills. Under the Eildon tree Thomas the Rhymer, alias Thomas of Ercildoune (Earlston), had his rendezvous with the Queen of Elfland. Before Sir Walter stamped his personality on this district, another Scott inhabited it: Michael Scott the magician of medieval renown, court astrologer to Frederick II the Holy Roman Emperor, whose death in 1450 he accurately foretold. Back in Scotland, the magician was plagued by a devil who demanded to be kept busy. Michael set him to split the Eildon hill into three peaks. The task was accomplished overnight and the three summits are there to prove it. Michael Scott then found his devil a steady job spinning ropes out of sand at the mouth of the Tweed. The Eildon tree is no more, but a stone marks the spot in the Rhymer's Glen not far from Abbotsford. Michael Scott is dead and buried in Melrose Abbey, and the devil, as far as is known, is still spinning ropes of sand.

The Border region, where people are heavily outnumbered by sheep, is a land of archetypal pastures and poetic valleys, of tweed suitings and cashmere twinsets, of rugby football, medieval abbeys, ballads of Chevy Chase and other murky frontier skirmishes, hints of Elfland and prophecies of Thomas the Rhymer, and memories of Sir Walter Scott.

Coastal scenery north of Berwick differs subtly from that further south. Tiny half-abandoned harbours are tucked like swallows' nests into the angles of cliffs, and smugglers' passages run inland from half-tide rocks. Places prominently marked on the map turn out to be sleepy villages with empty streets, huddled for shelter under a hill. Fragmentary castle ruins and broken footbridges decorate cliffs and offshore crags. One of them is Fast Castle near St Abb's Head, which figures in Scott's *The Bride of Lammermoor* and Donizetti's opera *Lucia di Lammermuir*.

The sea looks colder, the land more forbidding. Scots pretend to sniff a purer, keener air when they cross from England into Scotland. From the coastal route which is the Great North road, a major arterial route through Britain, the leafy lanes meander inland. Bordered by high beech and hawthorn hedges, they wander through a labyrinth of richly wooded hills and intricately winding streams from which the Tweed, Teviot, Ettrick and Yarrow gather their waters.

The horseshoe bend in the Tweed near Dryburgh has been dubbed 'Scott's View'. Not far away, on the Galashiels road, a tablet marks the spot where Scott, brought home from Italy to die in 1832, sprang up with a glad cry at the sight of the river. Along the middle course of the Tweed it is hard to escape the 'Wizard of the North'.

The principal towns are Galashiels, Hawick, Melrose, Jedburgh, Selkirk and Peebles. They cluster at, or above, river crossings and have built up a reputation for the weaving of high-quality woollen goods, especially the classic jumper and cardigan outfit. Parochial rivalries are sublimated in fierce rugby football traditions. A Hawick *versus* Gala clash is something of an Iliadic encounter and no one thinks it strange that places which would be mere villages in England (Jedburgh with 4,000 inhabitants, Melrose with 2,000) supply players to the Scottish international team. These players carry the goodwill of the whole region for, bitter as local antagonisms may be, all unite in the battle against the 'auld enemy' of England.

A stroll down a grey main street reveals a Border town's historical priorities. In Galashiels, a coat of arms on the Town Hall has the motto 'Sour Plums'; back in 1337, men of the town surprised some Englishmen eating plums in an orchard and slaughtered them to a man. Jedburgh's motto is the battlecry 'Jethart's here!' Magistrates there, they used to say, would hang you for stealing a sheep but not for murdering your mother-in-law; and 'Jethart justice' (execute the criminal first and try him afterwards) is proverbial in Scotland. At Jedburgh, in what is now a museum near the roofless abbey, Mary Queen of Scots lay sick after the harrowing 40-mile ride to see her lover, the earl of Bothwell, at Hermitage Castle. The exterior of the building, four towers and connecting walls, is still intact.

Selkirk, crowning a ridge above the Ettrick vale, has monuments to Sir Walter Scott (for some years the district sheriff), to Andrew Lang the author and to Mungo Park the African explorer, an impressive trio for one lonely Border burgh. Its most pathetic memorial, inscribed simply 'O, Flodden Field' recalls the dark day of 1513 on the slopes of Cheviot, when Scotland's army was annihilated and her king slain. Of the 100 men contributed by Selkirk, only one returned. The battle inspired the well-known lament, 'The Flowers o' the Forest'.

The land is rich in pheasant, hare and grouse. The Tweed banks above and below Coldstream (where General Monk in 1650 raised a famous regiment of Foot Guards) are exceptionally luxuriously wooded. Travellers along this chief Border waterway, princess of salmon rivers, navigate by dignified mansions, abbeys and prosperous farms. The river passes by haunted and hallowed ground: by ducal Floors Castle and Kelso's fine bridge, under Scott's View and Lauderdale, through the narrowing channel between Moorfoot hills and Ettrick forest, past Neidpath's theatrical ruin and on to the Tweedsmuir ascent where it rises.

BORDER ABBEYS

David I, 'that most courtly king of the Scots' (no mean tribute, coming from an English chronicler), employed his people not on fortresses but on abbeys. These included Holyrood in Edinburgh and the four graceful sisters of Tweedside: Jedburgh (1118), Kelso (1128), Melrose (1136) and Dryburgh (1150). The period was one of political stability, an interlude in the wars, and it has been calculated that two-thirds of southern Scotland's gross national product was swallowed up in the building of religious houses. David was a champion of enlightened self-interest. He wanted to make Scotland profitable and, having been brought up at the court of William the Conqueror in England, he wanted to civilize the country after the Norman-English fashion. For a start, he offered tax relief to lairds who agreed to 'dwell in a more civil manner, or be attired with more refinement, or be more particular about their food'. He persuaded Norman barons, friends of his youth, to settle north of the Tweed and set the locals a good example. From his reign dates the rise in Scotland of some famous families, Fraser, Lindsay, Lamont, Seton and several others. The surviving abbeys are monuments to this model of royal piety, son of St Margaret, and himself the bearer of the name Sair Sanct ('very saintly'). The abbeys were designed as colonies for monks from Cistercian and other orders in Normandy and Yorkshire, but fate decreed that for 500 years these magnificent buildings should know no peace. They developed no tradition of plainchant, illuminated manuscript or home-brewed liqueur. The Border abbeys' history is the history of military strongpoints on a bitterly-contested frontier, and their stones proclaim the turmoil of the border wars.

Above left Dryburgh, on the banks of the Tweed, grew rich in the Middle Ages but was later mercilessly plundered and burned by Border raiders. The picture shows the vaulted alcoves in which Sir Walter Scott and Earl Haig are buried.

Above right Jedburgh Abbey, in a town centre of hilly streets, is undercut by the swift Jed Water racing down to the Teviot and Tweed. It is one of the most complete of Border abbeys, though it suffered the recurring fate of large buildings in the 'debatable lands'. After the Reformation, when all the rich abbeys were dispossessed, part of the building was used as Jedburgh's parish church. The tracery of the north transept window is still intact, and the south-side windows still stand symmetrically along the nave.

Left 'If thou would'st view fair Melrose aright,
    Go visit it in the pale moonlight'.
So many visitors took Scott's *Last Minstrel* (1805) at his word that a sleepless custodian applied to have the words removed from the poem. Melrose was an imposing pile in its day, if the gaunt shell is any guide. An air of mysticism hangs about the tombs where Michael Scott the magician is buried, and an enigmatic inscription in the north aisle reads: *Here Lyis the Race of the House of Zair*.

Right Kelso Abbey, much knocked about, was further vandalized by crude restoration work. Now, stripped to its earlier condition, it is the most fragmentary but most atmospheric of the great ecclesiastical ruins.

Above Boxes of fish on the quay at Eyemouth await transport to inland towns.

Left For every thousand holidaymakers who speed into Scotland along the Great North Road, perhaps five turn aside to look at Eyemouth, one of the traditional bases of the Scottish inshore fishing fleet. Others are Peterhead, Fraserburgh, Buckie, Macduff, Lerwick, Ullapool, Mallaig, Oban, Campbeltown and Ayr. The whole fleet comprises 2000 boats, nearly all of which are under 23 m (75 ft) long, are privately owned and carry crews of about three apiece. The main catches are haddock, cod and herring. Herring catches are now limited in an effort to build up North Sea stocks, and so the landings of once-despised fish increase. The Scottish housewife learns to live with the cheaper mackerel and whiting. The Scottish fishing industry has gone through hard times since 1974. Many family businesses have had to be grant-aided and millions of pounds of public money are spent to keep Scottish fisheries afloat. If it were not for the solid stone cottages above the harbour wall, Eyemouth would resemble a southern Italian or Sicilian harbour where the boats and boatyards lie along an artificial canal with a protected exit to the sea. During a fishing slump in olden times the townsfolk turned to smuggling. A few of their subterranean caches and tunnels survive as reminders of days when, it was said, more people in Eyemouth lived below the ground than above it. The Eye Water, along whose tiny estuary the harbour is constructed, straggles down from a remote Lammermuir spring. The main road and railway between England and Scotland run along its banks. The more exotic 'sea foods' of Eyemouth include sea-eggs (found by skin-divers off the rocks) and Berwick cockles (found in the sweet-shops of the village).

Below The Tweeddale district has a number of mansions. Most are 19th-century enlargements of modest country houses. Bowhill (Duke of Buccleuch) commands the confluence of the Ettrick and Yarrow near Selkirk. It is much in demand for Game Fairs and the like.

Bottom Hermitage Castle above Liddisdale grows old sturdily after 700 years of violent history. The Earl of Bothwell acquired it from the Douglases, and here in 1566 rode Mary Queen of Scots to comfort her sick lover—a gesture which scandalized the nation. The rough trip almost killed her. J. M. W. Turner painted Hermitage and Swinburne wrote a poem about it.

Right Clartyhole is pseudo-baronial, pseudo-monastic, and 'the most incongruous pile that gentlemanly modernism ever designed' (Ruskin). It lies near Melrose on the Tweed and is better known as Abbotsford, the house Sir Walter Scott built. Here Scott died in September 1832, 'a beautiful day', his biographer J. G. Lockhart said, 'so warm that every window was wide open, and so perfectly still that the sound most delicious to his ears, the gentle ripple of the Tweed over its pebbles, was distinctly audible as we knelt round the bed . . . .'

DUMFRIES

& GALLOWAY

Previous page Mild temperatures, copious rainfall, shelter from northerly winds and accessible markets in central Scotland have given Galloway its landscape of arable fields and dairy farms.

Above The sale ring at Newton Stewart has in times past been a showcase of the black and 'belted' Galloway beef cattle. These are as highly prized among stock-breeders as the Angus and Aberdeen cattle of the north-east. An unusually high proportion of Scottish farmers raises and grazes livestock. Most of them have ample space to do it. The well-watered, well-drained Galloway hills have been the cradle of generations of robust animals, including the once common black, rough-haired Galloway pony. Now traditional cattle breeds are giving way before the heavier, more profitable Charollais and other imported stock. Grazing herds of belted Galloways, like bovine football teams in black shirts with white hoops, are no longer the characteristic sights of the pastures.

Right One of several natural curiosities in the deeply scored moorland neighbourhood of Moffat is the Grey Mare's Tail, a streaming cascade 61 m (200 ft) high near the summit of the lonely road to Selkirk. Ringed with hills at the headwaters of the River Annan, Moffat had its heyday in the late 1780s, when chalybeate springs were discovered. Invalids flocked to sample the waters, Burns and Boswell among them. Miraculous cures of sufferers from scurvy and scrofula were reported. But one wonders whether the disease might not have been preferable to the cure, for the taste of the waters was described officially as 'that of a mixture of rotten eggs beaten up in the scourings from a foul gun'. Baths, hotels, a *kurhaus* and assembly rooms were erected, but somehow the fame of this northern spa subsided, to be replaced in 1863 by a gold rush. Prospectors, amateur and professional, panned the hill burns and brought in quantities of yellow-veined rock. Miners trekked down from Fife with their picks. A nugget containing six grains of pure gold was found near the Grey Mare's Tail and exhibited at the Black Bull hotel in Moffat. Analysis destroyed all dreams: it was only iron pyrites, 'fool's gold'.

Dumfries and Galloway region partakes of the character of both Scotland and England. Visitors heading north feel they have already reached the Highlands. Those coming south have the impression they are already in the softer climate of England. The hand of the cultivator in agriculture and forestry is most evident in the landscape of a region designed, as the saying goes, to the measure of a man.

The composer Franz Liszt and the poet John Keats made a point of seeing this country. Each noted the bonny faces of the girls and the neatness of the villages. But the region has never known mass tourism, perhaps because most of it lies away from traditional touring routes. Travellers on its one major road to the north are too eager to make Glasgow or Edinburgh before dark to do more than salute the blacksmith's little house at Gretna Green, round which the shades of generations of eloping couples hover.

One historic line of communication passes through the region, the England-Scotland-Ireland link by the short-sea Stranraer-Larne route.

A corniche road, remarkable for its seascapes, embroiders the coast north of Stranraer. The mountains of Mourne and Antrim hills in Northern Ireland can often be seen in the distance, the latter only 40 km (25 miles) away. Ailsa Craig's solitary pinnacle divides the shipping lanes. The regional coastline is well furnished with topographical curiosities, from the hammerhead of the Rhinns of Galloway to the shallow crescent bays and estuaries of rivers.

Dumfries town, standing stolidly in the last bend of the Nith, does not lack literary associations. Robert Burns dissipated his final energies, died and was buried there in 1796. Hugh MacDiarmid (1892-1978), the only poet of international stature Scotland has produced this century, was born not far away. J. M. Barrie, the author of *Peter Pan*, went to school at Dumfries Academy. The home of the essayist and historian Thomas Carlyle was at nearby Craigenputtock, and the Maxwelton Braes of the song *Annie Laurie* were a little way up the Moniaive valley.

Within a slightly wider radius of Dumfries is the birthplace at Arbigland of the pirate and US naval hero, John Paul Jones. At Balmaclellan is the grave of Robert Paterson, self-appointed restorer of martyrs' tombstones and original of Scott's *Old Mortality*. The birthplace of Allan Ramsay (*The Gentle Shepherd*) is among the disused mines of Leadhills, the second highest village in Scotland. Along the western hills, familiar as the setting of Scott's *Redgauntlet* and *Guy Mannering* and R. L. Stevenson's *The Master of Ballantrae*, runs an open-air exhibition of Henry Moore's sculptures, one of the premier artistic attractions of Scotland's south-west.

The region's abbeys lack the ethereal grace of Dryburgh and Melrose, but they have had their share of ecclesiastical turmoil. At Dundrennan, Mary Queen of Scots is said to have passed her last night in Scotland (1568) before embarking on her weary years of imprisonment in England. Another 13th-century Cistercian foundation, Sweetheart Abbey, was designed as the repository of John Balliol's heart, by his wife Devorgilla. Devorgilla was the founder of Balliol College, Oxford. Their son John became a puppet king and a meddler in Scottish politics. Whithorn Priory, on a promontory south of Wigtown, rose on the stones of the first Christian Church in Scotland. Its most precious relics, the bones of Saint Ninian, were already a thousand years old when the bishop of Whithorn donated them to the Scottish church at Bruges in the 14th century.

The Glen Trool pinelands and the district known as The Moors are sparsely populated but by no means desolate. Not far away are valleys where azaleas and rhododendrons flourish, and the gardens of great houses such as Castle Kennedy, Ardwell and Logan are a generous tribute to the warmth and moisture of the climate. But the coast is bleak and salt airs stunt the vegetation. The setting is fit for the smugglers' tales which are so much a part of Galloway folklore. Here Sawney Bean, the celebrated man-eater, intercepted travellers. (By a confusion of myths he became Sweeney Todd, the Demon Barber of Fleet Street.) As recently as 1878, R. L. Stevenson was stoned in the village streets for some slight eccentricity of dress.

Times have changed. Car ferries shuttle back and forth at Stranraer and Cairn Ryan, the ferry ports for Ireland. Juggernauts with continental markings are seen on the road from Dumfries, and tourism is a growing industry.

Left This is not the botanical gardens of Palermo (Sicily has nothing so fine) but the environs of Logan House under the Rhinns of Galloway, a few miles from Scotland's most southerly point. From Portpatrick the Rhinns are a peninsula 26 km (16 miles) long and 3-5 km (2-3 miles) wide. Lord Stair discovered their subtropical possibilities when, in 1750, he laid out the Lochinch gardens at Castle Kennedy, close to Stranraer. Lochinch, Logan and Ardwell House make a trio of floral and arboreal brilliance, to which the Fishpond at Logan Bay adds a submarine touch. The tides come up a sloping shelf to refresh the sea trout which, conditioned by nearly 200 years of petting and pampering, will virtually nestle in the pocket.

Below The royal arms of sovereign Scotland (pre-1707) embellish Whithorn's Pend, or covered way, the entrance to a 12th-century chapel. The burghers of Whithorn say that the chapel stands on the ruins of St Ninian's 4th-century church, the first in Scotland. Eight kilometres (five miles) away on the coast of the moorland promontory of the Machers, the sandspit 'Isle' of Whithorn disputes this claim, adducing its own ruined priory and sculpted stones as evidence. Both Isle and burgh received eager pilgrims throughout the Middle Ages, but the burgh scored a psychological victory with a visit from James IV in 1497.

Left At Threave, near Castle Douglas, the National Trust trains its gardeners. This stunning layout of lawns and shrubbery is a foretaste, if you are travelling west, of the gardens of the Rhinns, 80 km (50 miles) away (see previous page). Tiny Castle Douglas is the chief town of Kirkcudbrightshire, which is not a county but a Stewartry, so called because successive monarchs chose a Steward (usually a member of the Maxwell family) to govern it.

Below As far back as 1220 the Maxwell chronicles mentioned Caerlaverock on the muddy Solway Firth below Dumfries. Battered and burnt-out, it is one of several noble ruins disturbing the pastoral panorama of the south-west—an example of the influence of history on landscape. England's Edward I, 'Hammer of the Scots', attacked it in 1300, and the Covenanters accomplished its ruin in the wars of 1639-40. These struggles decided that, whatever religion the king might profess, Scotland would be hardline Protestant. Old Mortality, the pious lunatic of Scott's novel of the same name, who went about tidying up Covenanters' graves at the age of 86, is buried in Caerlaverock churchyard.

STRATHCLYDE

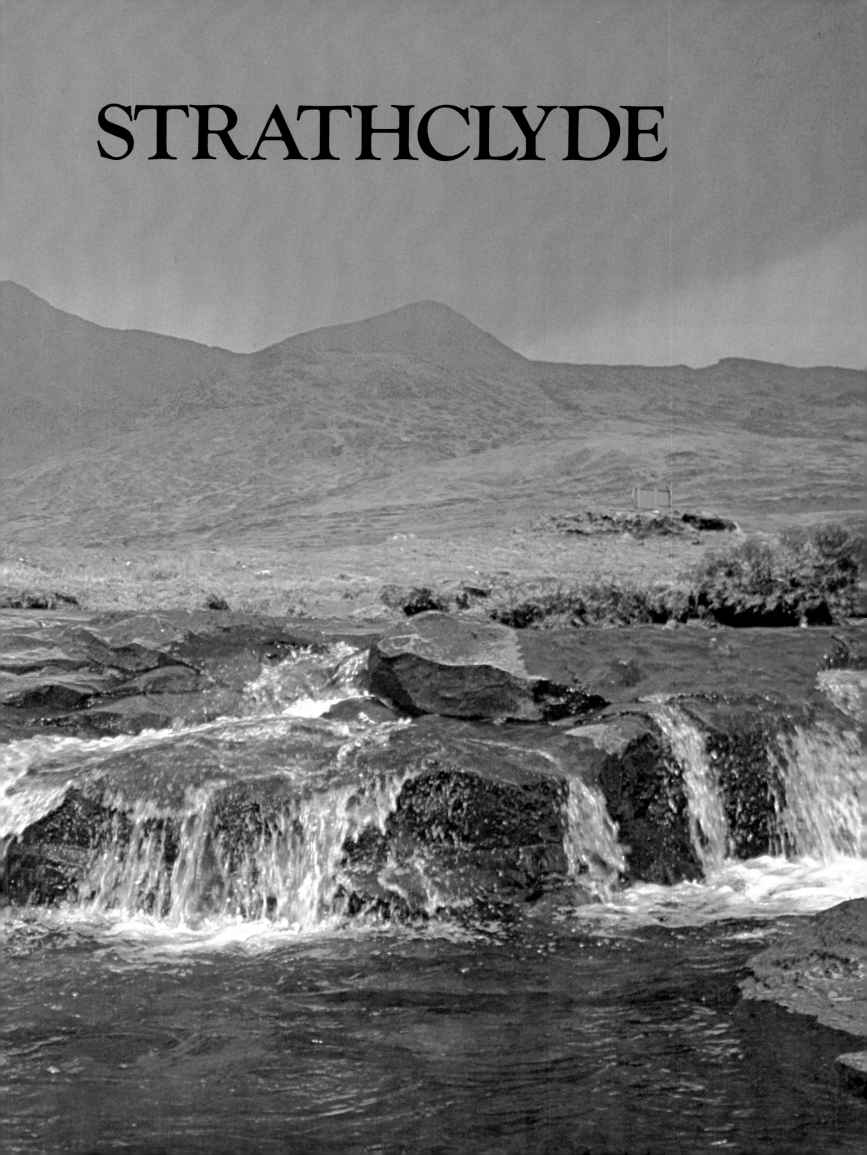

Previous page Aeons ago, Scotland experienced a series of volcanic eruptions. Floods of lava poured over the western Highlands and islands, smoothing out mountain summits and cooling on rocky tablelands. Today, short, sharp torrents uncover the underlying structure of the island of Mull.

Above The Mackintosh Library and the Glasgow School of Art, to which it is attached, are monuments to Charles Rennie Mackintosh. When Mackintosh died in 1928 his name was scarcely known, least of all in Scotland. The judgement of history, however, confirms him as an innovative architect, designer and painter, an artistic phenomenon shaken out of a provincial late-Victorian establishment. Deceptively plain kitchen cabinets by Mackintosh used to be broken up for firewood. Today they sell for thousands of pounds and the discovery of an unknown piece excites the art world. Mackintosh's Hill House, on the Clyde at Helensburgh, is a shrine for admirers. There is a Charles Rennie Mackintosh centre at Queen's Cross church in Glasgow and examples of his work may be seen in a city Art Gallery, the University and the Kelvingrove Museum and Art Gallery, all in Glasgow.

Right To most people, Glasgow suggests heavy industry, especially ship-building at Clydebank. Labyrinths of docks, basins and slipways congregate round the black, sluggish, astonishingly narrow Clyde. The river's history of commerce and war, adventure and exploration began when James Watt solved the steam-propulsion problem in 1765. In 1812, Henry Bell offered the world its first steamship service, from Glasgow to Greenock, in the three-horsepower *Comet*. John Brown of Clydebank built the large Cunarders—now this firm is the American-owned Marathon yard which builds oil rigs. At Scott-Lithgow (Greenock), Govan and Yarrow's, 'red' Clydeside's dream has come true, for all are in public ownership. Firms once noted for destroyers, submarines, cargo ships and dredgers have vanished or are diversifying into other specializations such as seabed exploration.

Ask a Scot if he comes from Glasgow and it is an even chance he will say yes. Glasgow no longer proclaims itself 'second city of the Empire', a title it once hotly disputed with Sydney, Australia. There has been a diaspora into new towns and the latest figures show it has fewer than a million inhabitants. But together with the shipyard towns and manufacturing conurbations up and down the Clyde, Glasgow still accounts for half of Scotland's population.

Glasgow sprawls over the middle belt of a region of mountain and flood which measures 160 km (100 miles) from the tip of the isle of Coll to just north of Cairn Ryan, Galloway. If this journey is travelled by road, rail and ferryboat it is more like 480 km (300 miles), so deeply penetrated and chopped by the sea is this country of Strathclyde.

Throughways lead the visitor west out of Glasgow to green and flowery sea lochs. The Clyde is an astonishingly narrow river, considering the vast ships which have been launched there. Along its south shore the view quickly opens on the widening firth, revealing a pattern of islands, and a chain of small holiday resorts separated from each other by prolific woodland and historic houses. On this route are Culzean Castle (a wing of which Scotland presented to General Eisenhower), the fog-free international airport at Prestwick and the championship golf courses at Troon and Turnberry. In this area are the towns of Ayr and Alloway, and the surrounding district is the homeland of the poet Robert Burns.

Once this green coast is left behind the visitor embarks on a voyage along the northern shore of the region. Here lies sinuous Loch Lomond, jewelled with 'those emerald isles which calmly sleep / On the blue bosom of the deep'. Between the serpentine lochs is the smooth ascent of Rest-and-be-Thankful and other ridges. From their summits all Scotia's grandeur seems laid out. There is the gnarled and twisted fist of promontory facetiously known as the Duke of Argyll's Bowling Green. An almost embarrassing proliferation of primroses, wild cherry blossom, bluebells and anemones is reflected in sheets of water of incredible clarity. The turreted country houses are immersed in drifts of daffodils at spring time. Strathclyde looks anything but a deprived region; if Scots of the western country could live on scenery alone they would be rich indeed.

A short distance upriver lie the shipyards which led the world technologically from the time James Watt of Greenock developed the steam engine. Henry Bell's *Comet* (her deck-planking now part of the floor of a Helensburgh hotel) pioneered steamboat services. But here, among the spring flowers and autumn heather and quiet waterside villages, we are in the country of Rob Roy, Allan Breck of *Kidnapped* and Para Handy, the coasting skipper popularized by Neil Munro. This is the setting of pastorales suited to Highland Mary, the Burns heroine of Auchnamore, and of clan feuds exemplified by the Dunoon massacre of 1646.

Strathclyde's offshore territories are those Atlantic barriers generally known as the Western Isles: Mull, Islay, Jura and others. To the west is also the knobbled Mull of Kintyre, almost an island, down which the tourist may travel 113 km (70 miles) and dabble his toes in salt water at every pause. Among village names, Tarbert is common. It comes from the Latin *traho* (drag), signifying a neck of land across which fishermen drew their boats to save a tremendous detour. These isles contain the dream homes of pop stars, Westminster politicians and northern industrialists, but sturdy islanders tend to resist sophistication and the froth of tourism.

Two islands, side by side but of different character, are most accessible to Glasgow: frowning Arran, rugged and mountainous, and smiling Bute. Between the latter and the mainland are the slender, rock-strewn 'Kyles' (straits). Bute's town of Rothesay is the traditional destination of 'doon the watter' excursionists from Glasgow.

In Strathclyde the sea is always a presence. From far inland can be seen the endless pageant of Clyde shipping (battle-cruisers and liners once, tankers and container ships now). Visitors may spend a whole day disentangling themselves from the skein of sea lochs and peninsulas to arrive at sunset on the Firth of Lorne. Here is the 'bridge over the Atlantic', a little stone bridge linking two points of land.

Left A new deal for weavers was offered at New Lanark in 1797 when David Dale built a barracks and a village round his textile mill, creating a kind of company estate on which the employees would live as one family. His son-in-law and successor, Robert Owen, sometimes called the Father of the Co-operative movement, took paternalism a step further by setting up health and education schemes for the work force and its dependants. He reduced the working day from 13 to 12 hours and did not employ anyone under the age of ten. His efforts made him extremely unpopular with other factory owners. Both mill and school are empty now, but the old, artisans' homes are being restored.

Above Since 1947, Cumbernauld and four other new towns (East Kilbride and Irvine in Strathclyde, Livingston in Lothian region and Glenrothes in Fife) have been created in Scotland. A Glasgow comic talks of 'deserts wi' windaes', and some observers say that the new towns prosper only at the expense of the old. But Cumbernauld has prospered, attracting 55 English and 29 foreign businesses, something the traditional industrial centres of Strathclyde would hardly have been capable of doing. New towns, growing to a fixed limit, are designed to take population pressure off the decaying hearts of Glasgow and Clydeside, while preserving a broad social balance. One-quarter of the homes in these new towns are privately owned, which is a high proportion by normal Scottish standards.

ROBERT BURNS

Shanter was a farm near Burns's native Alloway; and Tam was its owner, though his real name was Douglas Grahame. Burns's narrative poem *Tam o' Shanter* tells of this 'blethering, blustering, drunken blellum's' midnight adventure with witches and warlocks when riding home from Ayr market. In this poem Burns bestowed immortality on rustic expressions such as 'John Barleycorn' (whisky) and 'cutty sark' (a short-tailed shirt or petticoat).

Below right The painting above the door of the old thatched inn in Ayr's High Street shows a befuddled Tam setting off for Alloway on the eventful night.

Right One of the fine brass plates on the door frame leading into the Tam O'Shanter Museum (below right).

Far right The Ayrshire haunts associated with Burns are centred on Mauchline, near Ayr. Mauchline churchyard is the scene of *The Holy Fair*. Its old gravestones include those of Holy Willie and the subject of one of the most beautiful songs, Mary Morison. Burns farmed for seven years at nearby Mossgiel. There his plough turned up the famous 'wee, modest, crimson-tippéd flower' and the 'wee sleekit, cowrin'

Few people outside Scotland appreciate the intensity of affection which the Scots have for Robert Burns. To his fellow countrymen he is more than a poet. He is the champion of the underdog, lover of noble causes, hater of cant and pomposity, and prophet of a compassionate society hardly dreamed of by the philosophers of his day. Burns was condemned by some for the dialect he wrote in, but it masked a pure, smooth, lyrical talent. His homely phrases, such as 'a man's a man for a' that' and 'the best-laid schemes o' mice and men', entered the language and exalted both the Scottish character and the Scottish tongue. His love songs warm even cynical and puritanical hearts. His own murky love life and sordid end evoke a profound psychological response in those stern pillars of society (the 'unco guid' as Burns called them) who have always abounded in Scotland. 'He left his land her sweetest song, and earth her saddest story.'

Robert Burns (who should never be called 'Bobby') was born at Alloway, near Ayr, in 1759 and died 37 years later in Dumfries. For much of his life he was an unsuccessful peasant farmer. Poetry made Burns famous but never brought him real financial rewards. He depended on an appointment as Excise Officer at £50 a year to keep himself alive. He died penniless, from rheumatic fever, warning the doctor who came to see him that he was 'a poor pigeon not worth the plucking'.

A true national poet, Burns celebrated in song the streams and hills, the farmsteads, villages and village belles of his native land. The girls are in their graves, but the topographical features survive, from sweet Afton and bonnie Doon to the brigs of Ayr and the braes of Ballochmyle. Many a signpost on Scottish roads bears a poignant reminder of a Burns lyric.

Wherever Scotsmen gather, they celebrate the anniversary of his birth, 25th January, as Burns Night. The climax of the Burns Supper, and its speeches and recitations, is the serving of the football-shaped haggis, made from onion, oatmeal and offal. Burns's mock-heroic *Address* to this 'great chieftain of the pudding race' (*right*) is delivered when the haggis is served.

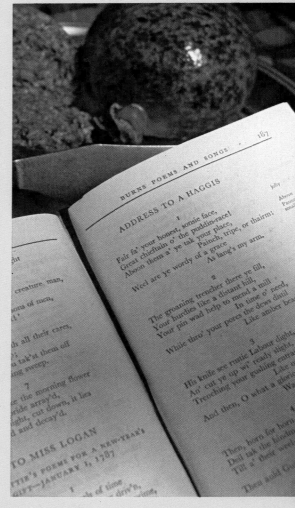

tim'rous beastie'—everyday events in the ploughman's life, but refined by Burns into poetic imagery and philosophical reflections. The poet's first serious love was a neighbour's daughter, Jean Armour. Her parents disapproved of his habits and poor prospects. When Jean became pregnant, the best the poet could offer was an informal marriage while he sought his fortune abroad. They were rescued from this fate by Burns's sudden literary fame. Burns wedded his 'bonnie Jeannie' at Mauchline in 1788. Their temporary bridal home is now the Burns House Museum. Close by is Mauchline Kirkyard in which are buried four of Burns's daughters.

The gardens of Crarae Lodge are man's answer to the hundred-odd species of wild flower which nature has planted on the mild, moist banks of Loch Fyne. Crarae, with its exotic assembly of blooms and shrubs and imaginative use of landscaping and colour, is a favourite venue for horticulturists' outings. It helps explain why rich English country-house owners through two centuries have sought for Scottish head gardeners. There are 24 km (15 miles' of magnificent scenery on the lochside road between Crarae and the head of Loch Fyne. In the seaward direction one can sail through winding sounds and straits for more than 112 km (70 miles) before reaching open water at the Mull of Kintyre. Across from Crarae Lodge there lives a clan chief whose name and address offer southerners a good exercise in Scottish gutturals: Lachlan Maclachlan of Strathlachlan, Castle Lachlan, Strathlachlan, Loch Fyne.

Left Oban is a ferry port for the isles and a collection point for cargoes of shellfish. Little of the town is pre-Victorian except for monuments such as the Dog Stone east of the bay (where Fingal tethered his mastiff Bran) and Diarmid's Pillar at the head of Loch Nell, where Diarmid the founder of the Clan Campbell (Dukes of Argyll) is buried. The impressive coliseum on the hill behind the town is McCaig's Tower. This is the unfinished masterpiece of an Oban banker who dreamed of immortalizing himself with a vast art gallery and museum. Bankruptcy cured his delusions of grandeur. McCaig's building plans also offered employment to people in Oban. Failure to complete the construction hastened the end of this new-found security. Thus, the portholed shell on the hill symbolises more than one set of ruined hopes.

Above Dr Johnson had his first taste of whisky at Inveraray Castle in 1773. He probably earned the refreshment: in that year Mrs Grant of Laggan, the Highland diarist, knew 'no road but the path of cattle' between Oban and Inveraray, and it is still an extremely roundabout route. At this principal seat of the Dukes of Argyll some ironmongery salvaged from the Tobermory galleon is kept, including a bronze cannon.

Right Tobermory ('Well of Mary') is the chief town and fishing port of the island of Mull. It is also the last stepping stone on the route to Staffa and Iona. Creels (also called sunks and lobster pots) are baited with mackerel and laid on buoyed lines on the beds of the island's lochs and sounds. The harvest of the sea-bottom is principally lobster, but scallop, squid and crab are also caught. Scampi fishing (Norwegian lobsters or Dublin Bay prawns) is a growth industry. After use, the creels must be scrubbed and perhaps tarred, and piled on the harbour wall in the sun and wind—only young, skinny, inexperienced lobsters will enter a smelly creel. In Tobermory Bay the Duke of Argyll and others occasionally go fishing for bigger game: Spanish treasure from the sunken wreck of an Armada warship which has lain under the sand since 1588. The ship is the *San Juan de Sicilia*, blown up on 5 November (a little ahead of the original Guy Fawkes Night). This was probably an accident or the work of an English spy, but certainly not the deed of gallant MacLean of local legend.

Above Mendelssohn's diary states 'What a wonder is Fingal's Cave! This vast cathedral of the seas with its dark lapping waters within, and the brightness of the gleaming waves outside . . .' The composer started roughing out a concert piece entitled *The Isles of Fingal*, which ended up as the popular overture *Fingal's Cave*. The island is called Staffa. It consists of basalt pillars which were stacked and jointed as they cooled from fountains of lava spouting out of antediluvian eruptions. Such landscape formations are well known to geologists, but they are not often so densely stacked and grouped on a shelf, surrounded by water, as at Staffa ('isle of staves') in the Inner Hebrides. The island is only 9·6 km (six miles) from the coast of Mull, yet it remained unknown to the outside world until 1772. In that year the English naturalist, Sir Joseph Banks, was driven off course on his way to Iceland and found Staffa the hard way—by running aground. The great grotto is 80 m (262 ft) deep and 20 m (66 ft) high. Local fishermen called it the 'musical cave' but Banks gave it the name of a mythical hero, Fion-na-Gael, or Fingal, whose adventures were chronicled in a poem of dubious authenticity by 'Ossian' Macpherson. Most distinguished travellers in Scotland in the 19th century made Fingal's Cave their farthest point north and sometimes waited for days, as tourists may do today, for a fair passage and a sea calm enough to allow them to scramble ashore. J. M. W. Turner, when a portly old man, jumped off the boat and spent three hours in the cave. While he sketched, an angry skipper and a boatload of seasick passengers rolled and pitched off the rocks, waiting for him. The result was *Staffa: Fingal's Cave*, a painting which fetched a big price in 1845 in New York. The poet Keats had better weather on the voyage to Staffa, 'for solemnity and grandeur it far surpasses the finest cathedral', he said. Jules Verne heard the Aeolian-harp effect of the air currents among the pillars: 'For whom do the wandering winds strike music? Surely this is the strange harmony that Waverley heard in his dreams?' When landing is difficult, modern motor-craft can at least lie close in, giving a sight of the cave's mouth, the tongue of hexagonal columns called the Causeway, and the Bending Pillars which, having lifted Staffa from the sea, appear to sag under the weight.

CENTRAL

Previous page Fighting and feuding, and even walking about, must have been messy occupations in the Carse (water-meadows) of Stirling some years ago. A 19th-century *Statistical Account* describes how 'thorough drainage . . . has achieved wonders. It is perfectly wonderful to behold how wet land is made dry and poor weeping clays converted to beautiful wheat fields. Where the plough could scarcely be driven for slush and water we now see heavy crops.' Stirling rose to its citadel from those marshes. It was a centre of strategic value in bygone days but now, like Perth, is something of a backwater. The castle looks down on Falkirk, prominent in the cast-iron trade and the aluminium industry; and on Grangemouth, once a drab terminus of the Forth-Clyde canal but today the principal refinery city of Scotland. Grangemouth has many ancillary chemical industries and a 92-km (57-mile) pipeline for crude oil from Loch Long in the west. For many Scots the old citadel remains nevertheless a metropolis of the spirit and some say that, if Scotland becomes independent again, Stirling must be its capital.

Above Highland dancing is an attractive sight and Scottish devotees compete for honours by dancing quickly and delicately over a pair of crossed swords in outdoor gatherings and indoor displays all the year round.

Right It is Scotland's boast that it had four universities (St Andrews, Aberdeen, Glasgow and Edinburgh) at a time when England had only two, at Oxford and Cambridge. But it is a far cry from the schools of the 16th-century Latinists and theologians to the progressive new University of Stirling, situated by the banks of Allan Water near the town. The university's MacRobert Centre (concerts, jazz, recitals, debates, avant-garde films and theatre) is open to non-students.

The wasp-waist of Scotland, from Grangemouth to Bowling, carries a disused waterway, the Forth-Clyde canal. This was a showpiece of transport in the pre-railways era. Engravings of the period show horses going at a gallop on the towpath and crowds of rustics gathering to marvel at the sight of boats appearing to sail through dry land.

The forts set up by the Roman general Agricola about AD 80, and the Antonine Wall which connected them 60 years later, are little more than a few dots on a modern map either side of the canal. But earth-shifters around Callander House and Rough Castle near Falkirk, at Bo'ness on the Forth and Old Kilpatrick on the Clyde still find Roman coins and pieces of pottery.

Traces of Wall and canal form the southern border for the Central region of Scotland, which extends to the 'bonny banks' of Loch Lomond, the ascent of the Black Mount on the Glencoe road, the Trossachs and Strathallan, and the short but impressive range of the Ochil hills. It is a small region geographically, but a populous one, and a nexus of routes. Central region comprises a little of the flavour and temperament of every part of the nation with inhabitants to match: from the Glasgow commuter and Falkirk foundry-worker in the south, to the grouse-shooting laird in the north and the oil technician of Grangemouth's refinery and tanker terminal in the east.

The Forth-Clyde belt was a cradle of industry, a hotbed of that Scottish mechanical genius to which engineering science is so much indebted. On the canal in 1790 Patrick Miller demonstrated a prototype paddlesteamer and in 1818 Sir John Robinson's *Vulcan*, the first all-iron ship, took the water. Iron foundries on the Carron river at Camelon built heavy guns for Nelson's warships; hence the term 'carronade'.

Central region is not all industry. As in Strathclyde, wild scenery begins on the very doorsteps of manufacturing towns. Stirling's cobbled braes ascend to a citadel which, like that of Edinburgh, accommodates entire regiments and dominates the land for miles around. Scotland's principal motorail terminus is in Stirling, with express car and passenger links from the south and west of England. So Stirling is the first Scottish town many visitors see. It impresses them with a sense of the past and allows them to map out their onward routes with the eye, wherever they are heading. The precipice walk round the castle walls provides a series of panoramic and historic views. From here one can see seven battlefields, including Bannockburn and Stirling Bridge, scenes of the victories of Robert the Bruce and his predecessor William Wallace, folk hero and freedom fighter. Visible, too, are Sheriffmuir and Falkirk (the sites of skirmishes in the 18th-century rebellions of the Old and Young Pretenders).

Under Stirling castle's fortifications and ramparts the river Forth meanders from its source in winding bends. Beyond the Lake of Menteith (one of only two lakes in Scotland—all the others are lochs) a bewildering tangle of far-off hills beckons to the west. Among them are Ben Lomond, the Cobbler, Ben Ledi, Ben Venue and Ben Vorlich, a foretaste of Highland grandeur.

From the same castle rock can be seen the Trossachs ('bristly country') and the skyline Duke's Drive winding down to the gap where Loch Katrine lies hidden. Nearby are Cambuskenneth Abbey, where the Scottish Parliament used to sit, and the Wallace Monument, a pencil of granite dramatically raised on a crag with the Ochils for a backcloth. Farther east, the rapidly broadening Forth carries the eye to the Forth bridges, Edinburgh Castle and Fife.

Central region is where Highlands touch Lowlands in clear juxtaposition. At one moment road and railway are gliding parallel across flat meadows; at the next, one is toiling past crags and the other is probing canyons where silver birches precariously hang and cascades of bubbling torrents throw up their spray. As the routes cross the Highland Line they face heather-covered moorland and make their way round the heads of glens which, years ago, knew no traffic but the flocks of sheep and their drovers coming down to the annual 'trysts' or markets of Stirling and Falkirk.

The hallmarks of Central region are, perhaps, the foothill towns of Callander, Doune and Aberfoyle. These are quiet, stone-built places, a trifle melancholy, but busy enough in the holiday season. With their country shops and war memorials, castle ruins and inns, they are a few miles only from the ironworks and refineries, but seemingly a world away.

If ever the ponds and lochs of Scotland are drained, the bottom will be found to be paved with curling stones. These polished, one-handled lumps of granite are often left out on the ice, only to sink in an overnight thaw. Curling is a uniquely Scottish sport (readily adopted in Canada) which resembles bowls on ice. Indoor rinks in ten Scottish towns engage the competitive fervour of men and women of all ages. Sustained frosty weather tempts devotees of the 'roaring game' (so-called from the hum of the stones in motion) to travel long distances for matches on the big shallow lochs. Occasionally there is a 'Grand Match', North of Scotland *versus* the South, with hundreds of players on the ice and the fun more important than the result. Here is a popular mass-curling venue, the Lake of Menteith near Aberfoyle.

Left Albion and Argyll, Arrol-Johnston and Galloway—Scotland entered early the motor-manufacturing field. It is said that 43 different makes of Scottish motor cars were exhibited at the Motor Show of 1928. Three years later the depression had swept all of them away. Vintage models, polished up and running smoothly, may still be seen early on a Sunday morning, out for an airing in the country lanes. They come from collections built up by enthusiasts such as the late J.C. Sword of Irvine, and now distributed among a few motor museums in the Lowlands of which this establishment at Doune, 13 km (8 miles) from Stirling, is an example. Farmland and moor are littered with priceless antiques from the dawn of motoring, if one knows where to look. A museum owner has restored vehicles from heaps of rubble: 'One was found under the collapsed roof of an old bothy—another had to be levered out of the bog with a telegraph pole—another had a poplar tree growing up inside it.' The museums restore modern cars too: classic sports cars which have crashed and been written off, custom-built station wagons abandoned in the glens and those competition models which triumphed in international events of the 1950s under the *Ecurie Ecosse* banner.

Left Exotic animals look well on a Scottish estate near Stirling, and on the whole they seem to thrive. A comprehensive collection of land and aquatic fauna, from lions to dolphins, inhabits this serene parkland round the mansion of Blair Drummond in the valley of the Teith. (For many years, before the expression 'safari park' was invented, Edinburgh Zoo with its free-ranging livestock anticipated modern anti-cage attitudes.)

Right Loch Earn, briefly glimpsed from the road north through Lochearnhead or traversed in its full length on the road west from Comrie, looks rich with promise although it lacks a robust mountain river, whose influx brings so many quiet, elongated Scottish lochs to life. Perhaps it is over-shadowed by the more scenic topography of the adjacent 'highland' corner of Central region and the more abundant foliage of neighbouring valleys. In any humdrum landscape it would be admired for its charms. The tourist authority has done a good job on the lochside road, providing delightful parking areas and picnic spots with rustic furniture for enjoyment of the scene from the water's edge.
The sheltered waters are ideal for aquatic sports, and several hotels in this district offer their guests sailing and water-skiing instruction. Lochearnhead is associated with Scott's *Legend of Montrose* and holds grim memories of the raid by the Macdonalds of Glencoe on Ardvorlich in 1620. A little way to the south lies 'Bonnie Strathyre' of the song of the same name. The dark hills to the west, thick with woodland and bracken, are the Braes of Balquhidder, for long the hideout, and eventually the tomb, of Rob Roy and his family.

FIFE

Previous page At Culross ('Coorus') in West Fife the past is more alive than the present—those bygone days when the gentility claimed a central reservation of 'plainstanes' and the common people went barefooted on the cobbles.

Above Throughout Scotland it is possible to eat lavishly. A sample can be tasted at the Crusoe Hotel at Largo, a fishing village and holiday resort. Here a juvenile delinquent named Alexander Selkirk grew up. He terrorized the neighbourhood and departed to sea. In 1704, after a quarrel with his captain, Selkirk exchanged the ship for the desert island of Juan Fernandez off the coast of Chile. He was rescued four years later, dressed in goatskins and surrounded by tamed goats. Privateering brought him a small fortune on the way home and he came back to Largo so richly dressed that his mother failed to recognize him. It is said that he spent his retirement living rough in a hut at the bottom of his garden. Selkirk's adventures were fictionalized by the author Daniel Defoe in *Robinson Crusoe*. This village gave birth to another historic sailor, Sir Andrew Wood, commander of the Royal Scottish Navy in the 1490s. One tower of his castle, and part of the canal he built in order to be rowed to Mass in his admiral's barge when too infirm to walk, can be seen at the foot of Largo Law.

Right Falkland, where rich and poor lived cheek by jowl, was a favourite residence of Stuart monarchs. The well-preserved palace rises amid the burgh rooftops, as centrally sited as the town hall or general post office. It has Gothic buttresses and arrow-slits, classical pillars and medallions, French renaissance towers and niches, but is splendidly Scottish.

'A beggar's mantle fringed with gold' was a Stuart king's description of Fife; the fringe being the relatively rich fishing harbours and ribbons of sand stretching all the way from Burntisland on the Forth and round Fife Ness to Abernethy in the Firth of Tay. Fife is sea-girt but the past century has given the region four magnificent communications links in the bridges on the Forth and Tay, not to mention Scotland's second motorway. Yet the 'beggar's mantle' remains surprisingly independent of other regions. Scots call it the 'Kingdom' of Fife. 'Fareweel, Scotland, I'm awa' tae Fife'—the cry of the Edinburgh fishwife on the ferry sums up an attitude of Fife's neighbours not entirely forgotten.

Many royal burghs, including the oldest in Scotland, Inverkeithing, grace the kingdom. Local pride paid a heavy price for the burgh charters, and the king who spoke of the beggar's mantle did much to make it beggarly. These royal burghs, many of them insignificant villages, constitute a collection of communities which use a harsher dialect, cultivate a narrower parochialism and stand on a more chauvinistic dignity than other areas.

Waterfront villages whose upper windows are darkened by the shrubbery of masts and rigging alternate with seaside resorts which will never be large holiday centres because they have no room to expand. But year by year they receive their share of holidaymakers and artists, most of whom would not dream of going anywhere else. Aberdour, a harbour with a history of shipwreck and murder, is commemorated in the ancient ballads of the Earl of Moray and Sir Patrick Spens. Above the silver sands near Kinghorn, another royal burgh, King Alexander III's horse stumbled and threw him to his death in 1286. Lower Largo to which Alexander Selkirk returned after a sojourn on Juan Fernandez, gave Daniel Defoe his model for *Robinson Crusoe*.

Unless it happens to be Open Championship week, stepping into St Andrews in the East Neuk of Fife is like stepping into a monastic settlement of the Middle Ages. Pointed windows, precarious towers, and the Gothic arches of a vanished priory are all that remain from a cathedral and a parish church of St Rule built in the 12th century. Rule, or Regulus, was a mystic who was led by a dream, according to legend, from the place of martyrdom of the disciple Andrew, at Patras in Greece, to plant the faith on these shores.

St Andrews has been a royal burgh since 1140. Its university, founded in 1412, was where John Knox, the Calvinist reformer, once lived. Ecclesiastical and academic associations still abound, but to many people St Andrews means golf. It houses the headquarters of the Royal and Ancient Club, the game's ruling authority.

Fife's hinterland has known poverty, not least during the depression years of 1930-33. In that time West Fife elected a Communist to Westminster. Mining towns still bear the scars of deprivation as a journey through Cowdenbeath, Lochgelly, Kirkcaldy, Buckhaven and Methil can show. Yet the coalfield country has its landmarks. There is Rosyth, the naval dockyard, which is now a refitting base for nuclear submarines. Upriver, the wynds and tumbled cottages of Culross are quaintly feudal. This was the scene of early experiments in undersea mining, coalgas production and other industrial techniques.

Dunfermline is enriched with Carnegie bequests (the industrialist and philanthropist, Andrew Carnegie, was born there in 1835). The fruits of these include a handsome library and a public park where peacocks strut through the botanical gardens. Six and a half centuries ago Robert the Bruce was buried in Dunfermline's Abbey church, and his name is incorporated in heavy stone letters in the battlements of the tower.

Fife has two faces. The more industrial one it shows to the south should not deter visitors from penetrating to the other side, to the rolling hills of the Howe of Fife and the somnolent villages of the Tay shore. Halfway house on such a pilgrimage might be Cupar, a thriving market centre with some quaint little alcoves and monuments; or it might be Falkland, where a royal palace is buried among other thick-walled, hoary buildings. The burgh of Falkland looks much as it must have done in the Stuart heyday. The palace was James V's last refuge after the collapse of Scottish chivalry at Solway Moss. Here, dying of a broken heart and hearing of the birth of his daughter Mary (1542), he foretold the dynasty's end: 'It cam' wi' a lass and it'll gang wi' a lass.'

Right Tom Morris of St Andrews was the greatest golfer in the world—until his son Tommy reached the age of 17, won his first professional competition and went round the Old Course in 47. At this time the fairways were unmown and the greens were cut by hand with a scythe. In the next year, 1868, Tommy won the Open Championship. He held the title for five successive years. The ornate red morocco belt heavily chased with silver, which he was given to keep, is now displayed in the Royal and Ancient Club House. Tommy died at the age of 24. Judging by the inscriptions on his grave in the churchyard next to St Rule's tower, and the wall tablet in Holy Trinity church, he was not only a golfing genius but also a most likeable young man. The four golf-courses of St Andrews (two maintained by the town council and two by the Royal and Ancient) extend over the foreshore links north of the town. Citizens played there as far back as the 15th century, nine holes out and nine holes home. This has been the accepted number ever since. The Bishop encouraged the players, although the law prohibited the game. Stuart kings preferred their subjects to practise archery. The Gentlemen Golfers of Edinburgh moved to St Andrews in 1754, and 80 years later it became the Royal and Ancient Golf Club. Those were the years when golf gradually established itself as an international pastime, when the manufacture and export of golf balls was the principal local industry, and the Old Course acquired its peculiar double greens (which still exist) to accommodate a tremendous influx of enthusiastic players.

Above The Royal and Ancient at St Andrews is the ruling house of golf throughout the world and the spiritual home of all golfers, whether amateur or professional. Its club house overlooks the Old Course, the most historic of them all, where for many years the annual Open Championship was held to determine the world's supreme exponent of the game. The club house is a treasury of golfing relics and portraits from the days when St Andrews was but a village.

Right A religious legend links Patras in Greece with St Andrews in Fife, and the X-shaped cross of the saint's martyrdom with the national flag of Scotland. Regulus, or Rule, the custodian of Andrew's bones at Patras, set out some time in the 8th century to realise his dream of a pilgrimage to the far north-west, carrying the bones of the saint with him. After a journey which lasted several years he took refuge in a seashore cavern, where another dream told him to deposit St Andrew's bones on a certain spot. He did so, then sought the protection of Angus MacFergus, king of the Picts. The spot is now St Andrews cathedral and Rule became its first bishop. Bones have been found under the crypt, but they have not been identified. Of bleached and breezy St Andrews, almost any legend would sound plausible. An air of lingering romance and decayed grandeur is natural to the place. It is small, but everything it has is of the best. The cathedral and castle are more impressive in their desolation than many large, well-preserved edifices. St Andrews university is the oldest in Scotland and its bicycling, scarlet-gowned students are most academic-looking. The spires of the town are more slender and fragile than most. Its ports and wynds are labyrinthine, and the little shops are quaint, like country shops. The ghost of the White Lady remains faithful to the ruined cathedral tower. Periodically she gives a moan in the direction of St Andrews Castle on the shore. The castle's defences are down and the stones were put to peaceful use in the building of houses. There is a Bottle Dungeon 7·3 m (24 ft) deep under the Castle's Sea Tower.

At one time East Neuk boats traded with Holland and Denmark, and East Neuk fishermen followed the herring as far south as Lowestoft. Fisher-girls used to go down on foot to mend their nets and cure the catch. The East Neuk once waged war on Lothian rivals and fought running battles at sea with lumps of coal. At this time there were a dozen little enclaves of coloured cottages with rusty pantiles and outside stone stairs, and no two windows alike, along the shore from Largo to Crail. The loud-mouthed 'cadgers' met returning boats and galloped off with cartloads of fish. The fishwives in voluminous striped skirts and bonnets trudged inland with their baskets of caller (fresh) herring, and their cries were immortalized in song:

Who'll buy my caller herring?
Ye may ca' them vulgar fairing—
Wives and mithers, maist despairing,
Ca' them lives of men.

Left Design secrets of the idiosyncratic 'Fifie' boat are laid bare in the Fisheries Museum at Anstruther, along with relics of historic voyages and samples of curious shellfish and conger eels.

Right Miller of St Monance has built 'Fifies' for 200 years. He supplied most of the 135 open boats of this matchbox-sized village's fishing fleet. Now he builds for overseas customers, and will make anything from a yacht to a minesweeper.

Below left Crail is the aristocrat of the East Neuk, the place middlemen retired to and built houses in, palatial by local standards. The devil threw a boulder at them from the Isle of May—you can see his thumbprint on it in the market-place.

Below In East Fife's fishing heyday, the tiniest village with the narrowest wynds, steepest streets and biggest fleet was Pittenweem, 'place of the cave' (of St Fillan).

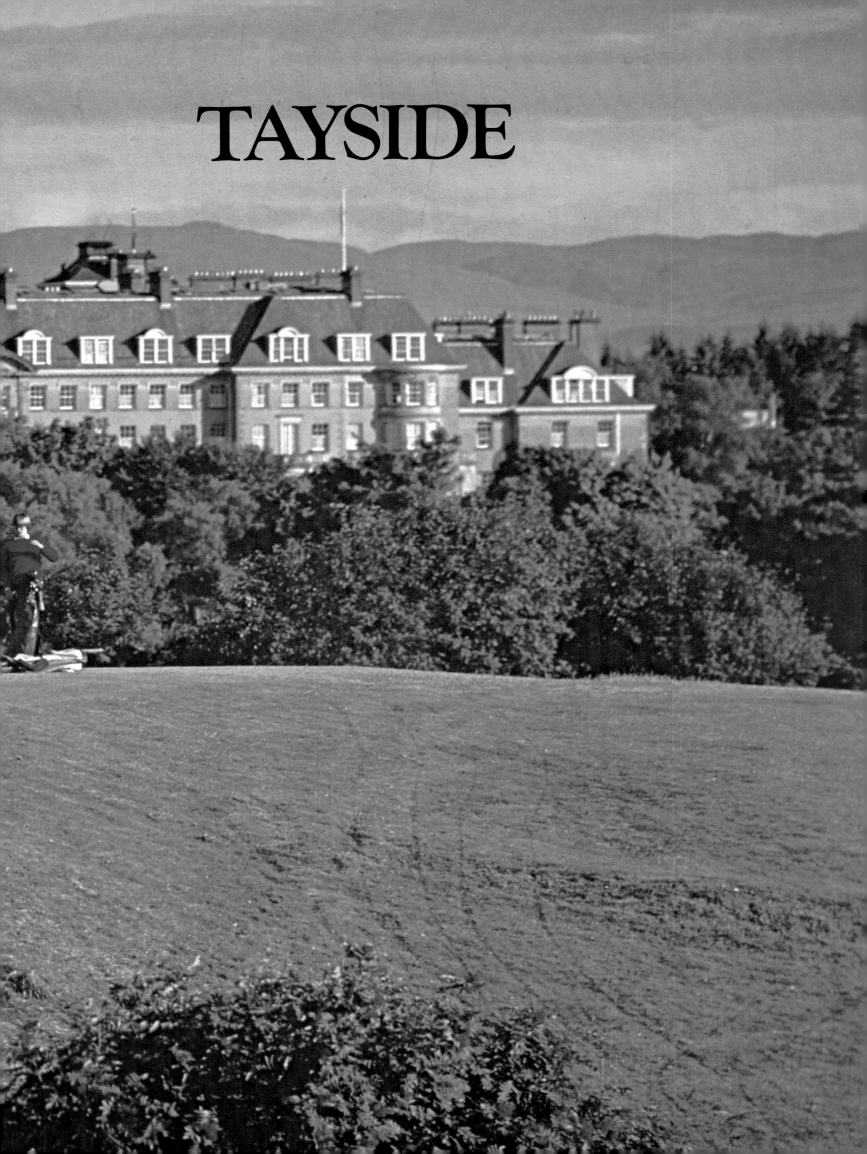

TAYSIDE

Previous page Most prestigious of country caravanserais, Gleneagles Hotel is a 283-hectare (700-acre) complex comprising luxury hotel, shopping centre, three 18-hole golf courses, railway station and helicopter pad.

Above 'Save the Little Houses of Dunkeld' was a National Trust appeal in 1956 to which the nation responded. The rows of cottages which were threatened with demolition were spared. On the route to the old roofless cathedral, travellers pass through what might be a Scottish refuge for Jane Austen characters. Here, 1400 years ago, there was an abbey church for Celtic monks. Count Roehenstart, killed on Dunkeld bridge in a coach accident in 1854, is buried just beyond the cottages. He was the last descendant of Bonnie Prince Charlie. Dunkeld's neighbourhood is bright with the variegated foliage of trees, particularly larches, introduced by 'Planter John' the fourth Duke of Atholl. Two decayed trees, an oak and a sycamore, at nearby Birnam, are said to be the last of that Birnam Wood which came to Dunsinane in Shakespeare's *Macbeth*.

Right Perth, the 'fair city', is a seaport, but only just. Below its trio of bridges the Firth of Tay becomes a serious waterway, but above them the Tay is shallow and canal-like. Who would imagine, looking at the river in Perth, that it is the longest in Scotland (192 km/119 miles) and brings a greater volume of water to the sea than any other river in Britain? The flood levels of the past two centuries are marked on an arch of the bridge and it is obviously for a good reason that certain quarters of the city are called 'Inches', or islands. Two stone bridges were built and washed away in Perth before this one, completed in 1771 and not substantially altered since. It gave the citizens not only a dry start to the north-east but also an escape from the claustrophobic gridiron of narrow, rectilinear streets in this typical medieval town.

Tayside region covers the sylvan Tay from source to mouth, and much more. One of its borders is marked by Rannoch station, a desolate point of no return for winter snowploughs on the West Highland railway, 27km (17 miles) from the nearest village. It is also bordered by Boar of Badenoch and Atholl Sow, two mountains which overlook the 459-metre (1,506-foot) Drumochter pass and the highest point reached by trains on British railways (the Perth-Inverness line). Other places which mark the borders of Tayside region are the Forest of Atholl, the headwaters of the Esk, Clova, Prosen and Isla, the terracotta-coloured cliffs of the Angus coast, the smoky seaport of Dundee, the city of Perth, the lake island of Loch Leven and the riverine lochs of central Perthshire.

Anyone who imagines Britain to be overcrowded should walk the upper glens of Tayside, the sheep tracks and cattle paths of the northern boundaries. On the Monega pass, a right-of-way into Grampian region and the Balmoral forests, the visitor soon finds himself at a height of 900 metres (c.3,000 feet) and the only hint of human existence is a shepherd or a shooting lodge on the skyline. Yet those same hills tumble into Strathmore ('Great Vale'), which is dotted with towns and villages, farmhouses and country castles, one of the most fertile agricultural and stock-breeding districts in Scotland.

Tayside gave birth to the affirmation of Scottish independence known as the Declaration of Arbroath (1320). The fishing port of Arbroath contributes 'smokies' (smoked haddock) to the Scottish cuisine. Its rose-red abbey's oriel window, facing the sea, once served as a lighted beacon for primitive mariners.

Sir Walter Scott used the legends and landscapes of the region in several novels, notably *Waverley*, *The Fair Maid of Perth* and *The Abbot*. The last describes the escape of Mary Queen of Scots from her island prison on Loch Leven. Roaming Strathmore and the sandstone coast one finds the homes of William McGonagall, eccentric versifier and reputed to be the world's worst poet, in Dundee and Sir James Barrie, creator of Peter Pan, at Kirriemuir.

In a field at Luncarty near Perth, the Scots king Kenneth escaped catastrophe on a dark night when a yell from an invader who trod on a thistle gave early warning of a surprise Danish attack. Legend says that after this event the thistle was adopted as Scotland's national flower. Another story, only hinted at in Strathmore, concerns the dreadful secret entrusted to the heir of Glamis when he comes of age, a secret so dire that he never smiles again. Glamis Castle, besides being the epitome of what most people mean by Scottish baronial architecture, has been a birthplace of royalty since Macbeth (11th century). Its most recent royal baby was Princess Margaret, born in 1930, the sister of Queen Elizabeth II.

The region claims the oldest tree in the world, a yew tree whose ramifications smother the little churchyard of Fortingall at the foot of Glen Lyon. Under it, or beside it, we are confidently told, the wife of a Roman centurion gave birth to the boy who became Pontius Pilate. Having accepted that, we make no great effort of credulity to see in the sculpted stones of Meigle, near Forfar, the lining of the tomb of Guinevere, faithless wife of the early British King Arthur.

The principal river is the 192-km (119-mile) Tay. This river, its hurrying tributaries the Tummel, Earn, Bran and Tilt, and scores of upland lochans (small lochs) and the busy little streams which feed them, are a paradise for anglers. The keen sportsman, however, may go through a purgatory of rough country to get to the best salmon and brown trout beats. Fat, pink-bellied trout are a speciality of Loch Leven near Kinross. During hard frost, the surface of this shallow exposed lake supports several hundred participants in a *bonspiel* or grand match for curling enthusiasts known as the North of Scotland *versus* the South. The market gardens of the Carse of Gowrie, along the Firth of Tay, and Blairgowrie are used for intensive raspberry and strawberry cultivation. This helps explain Dundee's pre-eminence as a jam and fruit-cake metropolis. The region has at least 50 golf courses, including championship links at Carnoustie and Gleneagles Hotel.

All this and the Highland Line too—this geological fault bisects Tayside, creating impressive cascades on some rivers and now and again a flurry of earth-tremors at Comrie. Tayside is a compendium of natural curiosities and covers the spectrum of Scottish life, scenery and character.

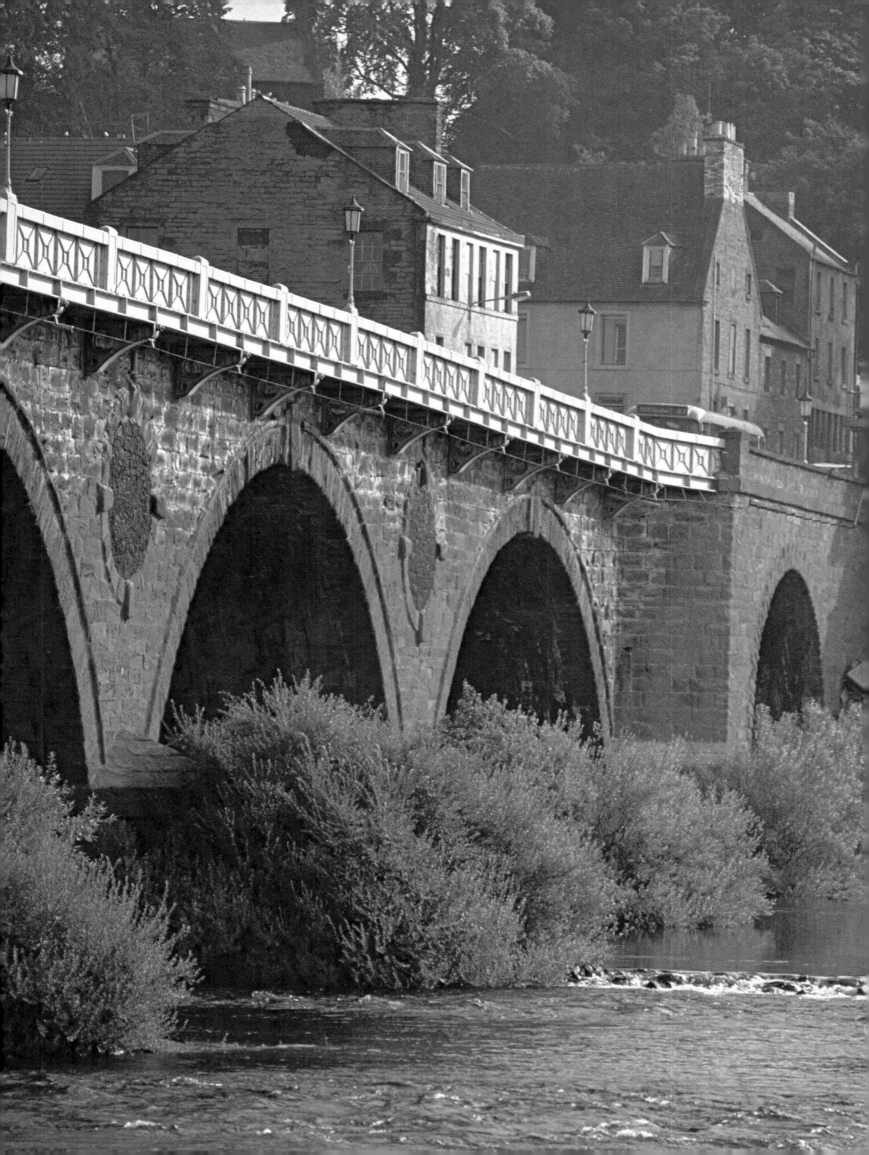

Left The run from Blairgowrie north to Braemar is one of the loneliest stretches of road in the British Isles, except on a fine, calm Sunday in January, when it is one of the busiest. Everyone is then heading for Glen Shee and the ski slopes which lie to the west, starting at the roadside, between Spittal of Glenshee ('Spittal' is hospital, a refuge for travellers long ago) and the Devil's Elbow which, when it was unsurfaced and narrow, used to be a harrowing ordeal for vehicles and their drivers. The Ben Gulabin ski lift goes up to about 762 m (2500 ft), where experienced skiers can either try the downhill runs or explore the hilly cross-country routes. Lower down, and near the road, the scene is busy and lively. Here, visitors who have never skied before, but will try anything, hire the equipment for an hour or two and initiate themselves the hard way.

Above When Lord George Murray, the Jacobite general, returned home to Blair Castle from the wars in 1746 he found the Hanoverian troops in possession. So he laid siege to the place, and Blair became the last fortress in Britain to undergo such an ordeal. It stands on the Perth-Inverness road and is the seat of the clan chiefs of the Murrays (Dukes of Atholl), and the headquarters of a private army, the Atholl (or Athole) Highlanders. In ancient times these ducal retainers fought under the fire-and-sword commissions awarded by Scottish monarchs to loyal chiefs. Their duties are now ceremonial and judges, admirals and generals are proud to serve as private soldiers in the 'army'.

GRAMPIAN

Previous page At Linn of Dee the infant river of Aberdeen bursts out of the Grampian highlands and begins its 120-km (75-mile) run to the sea. Here Lord Byron, poet and compulsive swimmer, narrowly escaped drowning.

Above July, August and September are the months for Highland Gatherings, a feature of the Scottish scene which has no parallel in other parts of the world, except for substitutes which Scottish expatriates started in Canada and elsewhere. In Scotland the Games have become commercialized. Hotel prices in the neighbourhood of Braemar rise steeply towards the end of August. Highland Games nowadays are by no means confined to the Highlands. They take place in Edinburgh, Glasgow and the mining towns of Fife. They can be spectacles of colour, music, competitiveness and excitement, but they do not pretend to be Gatherings. Students of Highland history do not talk of Games. The event is a Gathering, a perpetuation of the informal garden parties lasting several days which the chiefs held for their clansmen. People travelled long distances to the Gatherings, for the purpose of seeing the chiefs, and in order to be seen, showing their weapons and taking advice and greeting relations. If the more athletic clansmen liked to match their prowess in caber-tossing, shot-putting, hammer-throwing, mountain racing and dancing, that was incidental to the main business of the assembly. At the great Gatherings there would be found, and may still be found, several clans fraternizing—the Grants, Murrays and Farquharsons at Braemar, and the Lamonts, Colquhouns and Campbells at Dunoon (the Cowal Gathering). To enjoy a little of the authentic spirit of an annual Gathering it is best to choose some tiny place of old renown like Aboyne on Deeside, whose Gathering takes place at the first weekend in September.

Right 'Do not vaiken sleiping dogs' says the coat of arms over the staircase at Craigievar, but the injunction does not apply to the pipe band of the Gordon Highlanders.

74

The word Grampian came about through a spelling mistake, similar to those which have forced several etymological pitfalls on the stranger in Scotland (Dumbarton the town and Dunbarton the county, for example). Mons Graupius was the hillside where the Roman general Agricola defeated the Pictish tribes in AD 84. This was the greatest battle, in point of numbers involved, ever fought on British soil. No one knows where Mons Graupius is, though the likely location is near Stonehaven. Transcribing Tacitus, the Dundee historian Hector Boece (born about 1465) wrote 'Grampius' instead of Graupius. Geographers used the word to describe the flanks and spurs of the Highlands which descend to the vales of the Dee and Don and the stern headlands of Buchan.

The administrative region also takes in the southern shores of the Firth of Moray and the northern outposts of the 'roof of Angus' stretching up from Tayside. Two products of this countryside have carried Scotland's name to the ends of the earth: malt whisky, made in many distilleries, large and small on tiny, peat-impregnated hill streams; and Aberdeen Angus, the prize pedigree cattle raised on the green, granite-based farmlands.

If its recent rate of expansion is maintained, Aberdeen will displace Edinburgh as the second city of Scotland before the century is out. The 'granite city', as Aberdeen is called, is today a metropolis of oil and natural gas, a base for offshore technology and a new oil-related construction industry, and the pipeline terminus for the rich Forties field. Aberdeen's solid stone and hard-headed citizens stand up well to the invasion. It is still a seaside resort and the only changes old admirers recognize are a dearth of high-season accommodation and higher prices.

Westward, on one of the grand scenic routes of the British Isles, the visitor may follow the fast straights and sweeping bends of the Royal Deeside roads—'royal' because Balmoral Castle, one of a series of splendid turreted piles, lies at the end of one of them. Summer visitors sometimes see the royal family, perhaps with some political, diplomatic or military celebrities, going to church at Crathie, shopping in Ballater or attending the Highland Games at nearby Braemar.

Names of many Grampian rivulets will be familiar to whisky connoisseurs: Glenlivet, Glenfiddich, Glen Grant and the rest. Other streams attract the anglers and others the tourists for their rocky glens and boisterous waterfalls. Within 6km (4 miles) of Braemar are the foaming cauldrons of four linns (cascades): Quoich, Corriemulzie, Garrawalt and Dee. While convalescing in this neighbourhood in 1881, Robert Louis Stevenson wrote *Treasure Island*.

The mountains and cols which define Grampian's landward borders are modest on an international scale (Ben Macdhui, second highest in the British Isles, is barely 1200 metres (4000 feet). But the scenery has a dark and forbidding grandeur all its own. Corries (hollows) above the northern slopes of Lochnagar keep their snow all the year round. Through gaps towards the upper Spey Valley, in Highland region, go the wild and unfrequented drove-roads and shepherds' routes. The Lairig Ghru ('Gloomy Pass') beside Braeriach is part of a memorable two-day pony trek from around Braemar to the area of Aviemore. The Lecht motor road, steep, winding and exposed, rises to 610 metres (2000 feet) on its way to Tomintoul. It is invariably the first British highway to be snow-bound in winter and the last to be snow-free in spring. On many a Grampian walk, if destructive spates have not washed tracks or footbridges away, the rambler learns within the space of a few miles what is meant by Scott's 'Caledonia stern and wild'.

By contrast, the coastline of Moray and Nairn, plainly visible from the heights, is a strip of black pinewood and powdery sand-dune infiltrated by warm Gulf Stream currents. The botany of the area confirms it. For once, bathing in Scottish waters is no hardship. Cathedral towns and priories, golf courses, parks and stately homes rich with history seem always to be enjoying sunny weather.

The outlook grows bleak towards Buckie, Banff and Rosehearty. It is a dangerous and inhospitable sea trip to the herring ports of Peterhead and Fraserburgh and the cliffs of Buchan. Locked in their private inlets, insulated one from another, the fishing communities stress their individuality with an impenetrable dialect and a fondness for strict evangelical religions.

Below Few British cities have withstood the impact of violent change as successfully as Aberdeen. Grim under low cloud or sparkling grey in the sunshine, the city still looks impregnable against the technological assaults of oil and oil-related industries. Aberdeen occupies the undulating ground which divides the estuaries of the Don and Dee, the great north-eastern salmon rivers. It is the third city of Scotland, has a venerable cathedral and is a university centre, a holiday resort with broad clean beaches and a harbour which for centuries has exported the durable and attractive grey stone from which it gets its name of 'granite city'. Aberdeen supports a herring industry and a deepsea white-fish fleet. The port handles all kinds of maritime work, from dinghies to drilling rigs. The city is the chief port for the islands of Shetland.

Aberdeen's thoroughly modern appearance is deceptive. Ancient treasures are embedded in its canyon-like streets, where the traveller steps back in time from 'new' Bridge of Dee (a mere 450 years old) to Auld Brig of Don (more than 600). Envied for its success in developing ostensibly meagre resources, Aberdeen has acquired a reputation for ultra-Scottish parsimony, the kind of excessive penny-pinching which defeats its own ends—like the motorist who, to save wear and tear, switches off his windscreen wipers when going under a bridge. Every Aberdonian knows there is no foundation for the slur, and there is no evidence of it around the city.

Right There is no other town of real size in Grampian region. Inland from Aberdeen the oatfields and woodlands begin at once, thinning as they rise to the blue mountain spurs and stony glens. Below farmhouses like Provençal *mas* (defensive settlements) the people grow crops chiefly for fodder. The important business is the fattening of poultry, sheep and above all the renowned Aberdeen Shorthorn and polled (hornless) Aberdeen Angus cattle which provide much of Britain's prime beef.

 OIL

Little more than a hundred years ago, people in oil-producing regions bottled the liquid and sold it as medicine, seeing no other use for it. Then came machinery and motor-cars requiring fuel and lubrication and the Rockefeller fortunes were made. So rapidly did demand increase that, by 1919, fuel economists were giving the industrial nations another 30 years before supplies ran out. Since those days oil has been discovered in quantities undreamed of and the date of final exhaustion, at current and projected rates of consumption, has moved forward to the middle of the twenty-first century. Recently the politicians, economists and industrialists have transferred their hopes from land to sea.

Britain's oil lies in a straggling ribbon under the sea. It starts 160 km (100 miles) east of Dundee and runs north to a point 160 km (100 miles) north-east of Shetland. Along this line are about 70 exploration rigs, and a score of oil fields are already in production. Names of fields usually give a clue to their ownership. Shell/Esso favour bird names, for example Tern, Fulmar and Cormorant. Getty's Occidental compliments Scotland with Piper and Claymore. BP have adopted Scottish saints such as Ninian, Magnus and Andrew. Mobil and Phillips prefer women's names, such as Maureen and Beryl. Although the price of oil used for all purposes continues rising alarmingly, and the vision of a race of 'tartan sheikhs' in Scotland has evaporated, North Sea oil has enriched the economy and will do so increasingly for an estimated three or four decades. Britain's balance of payments benefits by the sum which, without North Sea oil, she would have to expend on foreign currency to buy the oil she needs. Secondly, huge sums come to the Government in revenue from licence fees for drilling, royalties levied on production, petroleum revenue tax and corporation tax. These sums add up to about 60 per cent of the petroleum companies' profits after allowances have been made for capital expenditure and operating costs. The third benefit, especially affecting Scotland, is the large number of well-paid jobs which have become available. There are jobs in rig, platform and module construction and repair, in specialist shipbuilding, in transport, communications and pipe-laying, and in professional and technical services. The pipeline terminal at Sullom Voe, Shetland, and the tanker terminal at Flotta, Orkney, employ more workers than the two groups of islands had in their entire populations before the oil boom. Grampian region, off whose shores most North Sea fields lie, now has less than half the national unemployment average, where formerly it had double. There is full employment in Aberdeen and Peterhead. Scotland's Atlantic waters have oil too, but the water is too deep for operations to be economic at present.

Left Like invasion machines from other planets, the oil rigs stalk the offshore waters of Grampian region. This production platform cost about £100 million to build, equip and instal. It is a metal island on stilts, semi-permanently planted on the sea bed. Its main deck is the size of three football fields and it houses up to 100 men who work a shift of 12 hours every day for two weeks, then go ashore by helicopter for a two-week rest. From the upper deck, 24 m (80 ft) above the waterline, it may be 198 m (650 ft) to the sea-bottom. The drill may go down another 3000 m (10,000 ft) to the pocket of oil which is trapped in the submarine rocks. The rigs and platforms are never quiet. They are brilliantly lit at night, and their flares and lights warn shipping to give them a wide berth.

If there had not been a fortress on the headland of Dunnottar, someone would have had to build one; so belligerently does the spur of rock advance from the Grampian coast just south of Stonehaven. One of the grand military relics of medieval Scotland, Dunnottar Castle has the history to go with the scene. It was a toll-gate and frontier-post from which the Keith lords, hereditary Earls Marischal of Scotland, commanded the eastern approaches. William Wallace captured Dunnottar from the English in 1296 and roasted alive the enemy soldiers who fled into the chapel for sanctuary. The armies of Balliol, Bruce, Montrose and Cromwell besieged it in their turn. During the interregnum, when Cromwell ruled in England, the Scottish regalia of crown, sceptre and sword of state now kept with other 'honours of Scotland' in the Crown Room of Edinburgh Castle, were brought to Dunnottar for safe keeping. Under siege, the starving defenders smuggled out the regalia to Kinneff church, where they lay buried behind the altar until the restoration of the monarchy. Twenty years later, in 1685, the witch-hunt of the Covenanters was on, and Dunnottar's deepest dungeon became a prison for 167 men, women and children. The victims lie in Dunnottar churchyard under the Covenanters' Stone. Here Sir Walter Scott first saw Robert Paterson, the original of *Old Mortality*.

WHISKY

Millions who will never eat haggis or sup on Athole brose acknowledge another Scottish product as an essential ingredient of gracious living. This is *uisgebeatha* in the Gaelic ('water of life'), anglicized as whisky. Fashions in spirituous liquors come and go, and different brands of gin, rum and vodka have their day, but whisky from Scotland has maintained a steady popularity and a respectable share of the market for 170 years. In the late 1950s it rose spectacularly to the top of the list of favourite prestige drinks throughout the world, and remained there. Within 20 years Scotch whisky exports increased sixfold. The distilling, blending, bottling, transporting and selling of Scotch whisky employs more than 20,000 people, more than the fishing industry. Home sales contribute £300 million annually in duty to the national exchequer and £95 million is raised in duty on overseas sales. For centuries a Highland drink, whisky is said to have been introduced to England, and thus to the world, by migrant Scottish doctors.

Below Visitors to Scotland might never notice a whisky distillery unless they were looking out for it. Some resemble insignificant factories, others are not much bigger than the bothies (farm cottages) in which whisky was formerly illicitly made. There are about 112 malt distillers in Scotland, though fewer than 30 recognized brands of 'Scotch' are on the market. The aristocrat of whiskies is the single malt, or unblended spirit, produced only in Scotland, and for a long time despised in the south on account of its watery appearance and occasionally smoky flavour. The single malts are today the connoisseurs' whiskies. They cost half as much again as blended Scotch. About 40 malt distilleries cluster along Speyside in the Grampian hills, north-west of Aberdeen, and

seven of them are in the village of Dufftown (population 1400) near the foot of Glenfiddich. In this bonded warehouse the precious liquid matures. In ten or twelve years' time (maybe twenty-one years but never less than seven) it will be on sale as Glenfiddich malt whisky.

Right Much whisky was made illicitly and the memoirs of Highland lairds recall nostalgically the mountain huts with their well-built stone walls, watertight thatches, arrays of casks and tubs, and iron pipes leading the cold spring water to the still-rooms. The permanence of the layout showed that the one-man distillery stood in little danger of the law. Maltster and excise officer were generally on the best of terms, for the latter, appointed to his job for life, soon

learned discretion if he wanted to live peaceably among his neighbours. It is a far cry from the old lawless days to the strictly controlled operations of modern times, the hygienic environment and sophisticated equipment of the still-rooms and vats of Speyside, exemplified by this scene of the Glenfiddich distillery. But the 'mountain dew' which comes out in the end is fundamentally the same as it has always been.

Above Apart from burn water, the basic ingredient of whisky is malted barley. The fields of waving grain seen in the agricultural regions of Scotland in summer are more likely to be going into whisky than into bakery produce. This is some of the raw material which pours into a storehouse on the Dufftown-Tomintoul road, where the Livet Water rushes down from the Banffshire highlands to join the Avon and the Spey. The end-product is Glenlivet whisky, usually referred to as *the* Glenlivet—a spirit of such refined purity and concentrated stability that almost all blended whiskies contain a proportion of it. Australia, the United States, Brazil, Spain and Japan are among the importers of malt spirit in bulk. As the Scottish distillers are fond of pointing out, it has done a lot to make the *parvenus* liquors of those countries acceptable to people who cannot get hold of the real stuff.

Several Scottish distillers open their premises to visitors; and on Speyside the Tourist Board has established an instructional Whisky Trail.

HIGHLAND

Previous page A flotilla of islets, anchored for eternity. Highland scenery achieves its greatest splendour and tranquillity at Badcall Bay in north-west Sutherland. Beyond lies Lewis and, beyond that, America.

Above The Duke of Portland, up at Langwell in Caithness, disliked railways. This is why the main line to Wick makes an elaborate detour round the grouse moors and deer forests. The Duke of Sutherland, 32 km (20 miles) south at Dunrobin Castle (above), was fond of them and so, in Sutherland, the trains followed the road past Dunrobin. In fact, trains so fascinated the first Duke that when he turned his 13th-century seaside ruin into a Victorian extravaganza (with more rooms than any hotel in Scotland), he operated his own railway, fully equipped and staffed, in the park. Beinn a' Braghie rises 305 mm (1000 ft) above Dunrobin Glen. To reach the statue of the first Duke on its summit was a test of the strength and power of vehicles in pioneering motoring days.

Right An earlier Dunrobin must have looked something like Eilean Donan Castle in the western Highlands. The castle has been restored and has a causeway to the Glen Shiel shore. The castle is inhabited again and much in demand by outdoor-fashion photographers and makers of Bonnie Prince Charlie films. (The Prince was never there, but the castle did have the distinction of being bombarded by a Royal Navy frigate during an abortive Spanish-Jacobite invasion in 1719.)
Eilean Donan and Loch Duich are close to journey's end on one of the Roads to the Isles which Doctor Johnson and Boswell travelled in 1773. Clach Johnson, a boulder in Glen Shiel a short distance east, is shown to the credulous as the spot where Johnson decided to write his classic literary work of Scottish travel, *A Journey to the Western Isles*.

'If you'd seen these roads before they were made,/You would lift up your hands and bless General Wade.' Wade and his successor Caulfield (who wrote the couplet) did more than Sir Walter Scott to open the way to the Highlands. Modern roads follow the robust foundations and the sturdy high-arched bridges these two military engineers built in the 1740s. The Highlandman, so heavily romanticized, remained for more than a hundred years afterwards untouched by social progress. Ignorance, filial obedience to the clan chief and a capacity for enduring hardship were his characteristics. The MacPhersons once complained of their laird's effeminacy when they saw him brush snow off a stone before taking it for his pillow.

This primitive simplicity was first disturbed when the great landowners discovered that sheep were more profitable than cattle, and instituted the Clearances which forced the crofters to emigrate. The way these frugal and industrious exiles succeeded in the New World is as remarkable as the way they kept their love of Scotland.

The great surprise for visitors is the changing scenery of northern Scotland. One may pass from heather, bracken and springy turf to granite rock and bog, to serrated peak and snow-water lake, petrified forest and the archaic rock of Assynt, to the red Torridon sandstone of Wester Ross and the flowery land of Lochs Maree and Ewe. The black rocks of the Coolins on Skye, and of the Outer Hebrides, lie like basking whales on the horizon. Sea inlets grow ever deeper and more fiord-like. Cliffs on which the quartzite gleams above crescents of firm sand lead round Sutherland to Caithness, a windswept moorland county of Norse place-names.

The northern archipelagos, two groups of about 200 isles (40 inhabited), are also linked historically and geographically with Scandinavia. A resident of Haroldswick in Shetland, applying for a travel allowance and required to state the nearest railway station, wrote quite correctly 'Bergen' (Norway).

'Shetland for scenery, Orkney for antiquities' the saying goes, and both for bird-watching. Snowy owls, phalaropes, waders and divers, wheatears, shearwaters and Arctic terns, skuas, auks and kittiwakes nest in immense colonies on the stack rocks. A score of promising oil and natural gas fields, and two big terminals, Sullom Voe in Shetland and Flotta in Orkney, on which the pipelines converge, bring immigrant hordes of human beings. But they are an insignificant handful compared with the migratory swarms of many species of birds.

Golden eagles and equally spectacular ospreys can be seen in the west and central Highlands in protected habitats. The deer population is said to be denser than anywhere else in the world and it increases, despite the growing interest in stalking. Belgian, French and German businessmen pay up to £200 a day to participate in this pursuit.

Western islanders and Highlandmen speak Gaelic, a language akin to Erse, Welsh and Manx. There is no universally agreed grammar. The current dictionary dates from 1845 and not all the 90,000 Gaelic speakers in Scotland understand each other. Haunting love songs, chiefly associated with the Harris wool spinners and weavers in Hebridean crofts, are Gaelic's contribution to the nation's cultural heritage. Highland region and the Islands are rich in ancestral memories and their art and architecture are of a primitive nature.

Most popular with tourists are Inverness and the Great Glen, where visitors gaze hopefully at the supposed lair of the Loch Ness monster, first 'sighted' in 1932. A new bridge on the Inverness Firth will, in 1981, disclose the charms of the Black Isle. This is neither black nor an island, but a mild countryside in quiet harmony with nature.

Many a country house near Inverness preserves undisturbed the room in which Prince Charles Edward, the Stuart pretender, slept on the night before Culloden in 1746. Post-Jacobite romantics, especially the women, represent the encounter as a betrayal of old values and the undoing of Scotland. On a misty evening on the road over Culloden Moor, where the memorial stones lean in clumps of gorse, even the cynic feels a sentimental sympathy for the lost cause and the death of Stuart hopes. The subsequent wanderings of the young Prince through the western Highlands add something to the glamour of the routes we follow today.

Despite its harsh weather, the Highland region has long been associated with outdoor pursuits. It provides a necessary hunting and fishing ground for its inhabitants, and is a grand sporting arena for climbers, skiers, shooting and deer-stalking parties, naturalists, curlers, pony-trekkers and devotees of esoteric rustic contests and trials of strength.

Left The ridges which rise above Glenmore, and the isolated peaks of the Cairngorm and Monadhliath massifs and Grampian highlands, are regarded as training grounds for climbers with Himalayan ambitions. These ridges and peaks are of relatively low altitude, the highest mountain (the second highest in Britain) rising to only 1309 m (4296 ft). Yet conditions may resemble those which mountaineers encounter in Nepal and Kashmir. Although it is possible to stroll up on a track which motor cars have used, and be at the summit in a few hours, it is also possible to take the alternative route. This has tortuous and exhausting snow-climbs of a steepness and complexity unknown elsewhere on this side of the Matterhorn.
Scotland's highest mountains after Ben Nevis are grouped in the blue majestic Cairngorms, around Cairn Gorm itself (but Ben Macdhui is the

highest). Here, too, are clustered the densest concentrations of 'Munros'. These 1000-m (3000-ft) peaks are named after the enthusiast who climbed them all. Thanks to road improvements between Aviemore and Glenmore Lodge, energetic walkers can accomplish both Ben Macdhui and Cairn Gorm in one day, using Glenmore and the Lairig Ghru, and the magnificent plateau walk between the summits.

Below left An athlete at Glenfinnan, archetypal Highland Games setting at the head of a loch in the natural amphitheatre of the hills, exerts himself. Here, in the hopeful days of August 1745, Prince Charles Edward raised his standard. The monument, erected by the local laird, pays homage to those clansmen who followed him down the trail to Culloden Moor. When telegraphic communications first came to the north, engineers could never understand why the poles went missing. They happened to be the right size for the ancient pastime of tossing the caber. The idea is to run with it and, with a combination of brute strength and a twirl, to launch it forward so that it topples over on end. This feat is greeted with acclaim at Highland Games, for contestants fail much more often than they succeeed.

Below right Glencoe, 'glen of weeping', sombre with memories of the massacre of 1692, has blossomed out as one of the three winter playgrounds of Scotland. The other two are Glen Shee and the Cairngorms. Touristic developments under the high massifs have been a blessing to rock climbers and hill walkers, but they have revolutionized winter sports. Only 50 years ago an Englishman with skis in the Highlands was liable to be asked what the planks were for. Nowadays the schools teach skiing and lowland cities have their 'dry' nursery slopes. The railway station platform at Aviemore when the London-Inverness train pulls in is reminiscent of Grindelwald, and numerous Swiss and Austrian instructors are finding rewarding careers in the budding complexes of the Scottish snow country.

BONNIE PRINCE CHARLIE

With the death of Queen Anne, in 1714, a dynasty ended and the Hanoverian monarchs came to the British throne. But a Stuart line survived through the offspring of James VII of Scotland (James II of England). His son, the Old Pretender, in 1715 and his grandson, the Young Pretender, in 1745 tried to assert their claims with the aid of a predominantly Scottish following.

Prince Charles Edward Stuart, the Young Pretender or 'Young Chevalier', owed his chance to the French, who were at war with Britain and seeking a diversion. He landed on Eriskay, in the Outer Hebrides, with a few companions and set up his standard in Glenfinnan (Fort William-Arisaig road) in August 1745. Marching south, the small army took Edinburgh by surprise, occupied the Palace of Holyroodhouse and proclaimed the Prince's father King James VIII. Royalist forces rallied, but the Jacobites brushed them aside at Prestonpans, East Lothian. They marched south towards London, gathering followers as they went. Why Prince Charles turned his army back at Derby, 225 km (140 miles) from the capital, and whether he was wise to do so, are questions still debated by historians.

Hanoverian troops under the Duke of Cumberland started in pursuit and the two forces fought half-heartedly at Falkirk in January 1746. The Jacobites continued retreating north, short of food, increasingly demoralized and diminished by large numbers deserting to their homes as the spring sowing season came round. The Redcoats caught up with them at Culloden. After his defeat, Prince Charles Edward escaped and became a fugitive in the western Highlands and the Hebrides for five months. He was guided and protected by Flora Macdonald, a 19-year-old girl from South Uist. The French eventually rescued the Prince from Borrodale, close to where he had hoisted his standard the previous year. Driven from Paris under the terms of the Anglo-French peace treaty, he set up house in Rome. Faithful old friends bore stoically with his arrogance and chronic alcoholism, while in Scotland the romantic legend of the 'king over the water' took root. Harsh reprisals against former Jacobites only perpetuated it. A hundred years later, old-fashioned lairds were still passing their glasses over a decanter of water when they drank the King's health; and Georgian wits recited the toast: "God bless the King—I mean the Faith's Defender/God bless (no harm in blessing) the Pretender/But which the former is, and which the latter/God bless us all! That's quite another matter."

On Culloden Moor near Inverness, 25-year-old Charles Edward Stuart (left), a man of courageous Scottish energy mixed with some Polish blood and spurious Italian charm, faced 25-year-old Cumberland. Cumberland was British but with strong German connections. He was a serious military tactician. In 40 minutes 9000 Redcoats had routed 5000 Jacobites and left about 1000 dead on the moor.

Right The Highlanders' graves, grouped according to their clans, form a rough semi-circle opposite the principal cairn.

Far left The Old Leanach farmhouse survived the fighting and is now cared for by the National Trust for Scotland.

THE BATTLE
OF CULLODEN
WAS FOUGHT ON THIS MOOR
16TH APRIL 1746.
THE GRAVES OF THE
GALLANT HIGHLANDERS
WHO FOUGHT FOR
SCOTLAND & PRINCE CHARLIE,
ARE MARKED BY THE NAMES
OF THEIR CLANS.

Above Looking much as it did in the Young Pretender's day, Moil Castle commands the narrows by which travellers pass 'over the sea to Skye'. Its original owner was a Danish noblewoman to whom the Gaels gave the name Saucy Mary. She stretched a chain to the mainland and demanded toll from the passing ships. The Young Pretender took refuge on Skye after he and his troops were routed at Culloden.

Below Very old inhabitants call them the 'long island', but to modern geography they are the Outer Hebrides. This is a kite-shaped group of islands 193 km (120 miles) long from Lewis and Harris, the cloth-weaving isles, down through the tapering tail of the Uists, Benbecula and Barra, to the fluttering fragments of Vatersay, Sandray, Berneray and others. Here lies the north-west frontier of civilized Europe. This is where the millionaire Lord Leverhulme, coming into possession of Lewis in 1918, poured a fortune into various schemes to improve the economy, and retired defeated by local apathy. Sheep have to be cleared off the runway to permit the aircraft from Glasgow to land. The *Politician*, with a huge cargo of whisky, went aground on the Eriskay rocks in 1941 and gave Compton Mackenzie the idea for the popular novel and movie *Whisky Galore*.

'Black houses' survive on the smaller isles. These are cottages of undressed boulders, sometimes built half underground and sheeted down with a dense straw thatch. Modifications to the outline, such as windows, chimneys and a paved floor, make this South Uist cottage very attractive.

Bottom On the west coast of the island of Lewis, near the head of Loch Roag, the Standing Stones of Callanish indicate that neolithic man was a resident of the Hebridean islands. One large cairn is encircled by 13 monoliths, and other stones which may have formed concentric circles are dotted about. There is a 'broch' (cylindrical stone tower of Pictish origin) a short distance away.

Right Barra, the windswept island, lies in the mainstream of the Gaelic language, folksong and legend. Kishmul Castle, built about 1430 by Barra's overlords, the MacNeils, is said to be the biggest ancient monument in the Hebrides. It protects the entrance to the island's only sheltered harbour, Castlebay. Southward in Berneray, the lighthouse on Barra Head stands 178 m. (583 ft) above the sea, with the greatest arc of visibility in the world.

Cartographical convenience usually dictates that Orkney and Shetland are tucked away in a corner of Scotland's map, often on a reduced scale; and the spread of latitude they cover is not appreciated. If they were inverted they would stretch from the Pentland Firth to Perth.

Left Lerwick, capital of Shetland and the most northerly town in the British Isles, is a jumble of cottages and alleyways which seem to have been tipped by accident on to the strand. But in the season the harbour is crammed with drifters and trawlers, and foreign accents from Spain to the Soviet Union are heard. The visitors, along with sea-angling tourists and oilmen from the Sullom Voe terminal, bargain for Fair Isle shawls and sweaters in unpretentious shops.

Main picture Stromness is on Orkney's largest island, known as the 'Mainland', and has a typical treeless landscape. It is a stone's-throw from the late Stone Age settlements of Maeshowe, Stenness and Skara Brae. It closes the northern exits from the former warbase of the British fleet in Scapa Flow.

INDEX

Page numbers in italics
refer to illustrations

Acknowledgements

The publishers would like to thank the following individuals and organizations for their kind permission to reproduce the photographs in this book:

Photographs supplied by the Scottish Tourist Board 8-9, 11, 14-15, 16 left, 16-17, 20, 22 below, 24-25, 25 right, 26 above, 26-27, 28-38, 42-49, 52, 54-55, 60, 62 above, 64 below left, 70-77, 78-79 below left, 90-91 above-95

Special photography by Mike St. Maur Sheil Title Page, 10, 18-19, 21, 22 above, 23 above and below, 26 below, 39-41 right, 50-51, 53, 56 above-59, 61, 62 below-64 above, 64-65 below-69

Bruce Coleman Ltd. (Nelly Peter) Half Title; Tim Graham 6-7, 77 right; The National Portrait Gallery, London 12 below, 13, 90 below right; Mike St. Maur Sheil 65 above; Kim Sayer Endpapers; Spectrum Colour Library 12 above

The publishers would also like to thank The Scotch House, Knightsbridge, London for providing the tartans for the endpaper photograph

PDO 82-1307